T0169496

VANCOUVER
ALIVE AT THE CENTER

Vancouver
Alive at the Center

Comtemporary Poems from
Vancouver, British Columbia

Vancouver

Edited by

Daniela Elza
Bonnie Nish
Robin Susanto

OOLIGAN
PRESS

Vancouver: Alive at the Center
Contemporary Poems from Vancouver, British Columbia
© 2013 Ooligan Press

ISBN13: 978-1-932010-53-4

Ooligan Press
Department of English
Portland State University
P.O. Box 751, Portland, Oregon 97207
503.725.9410 (phone); 503.725.3561 (fax)
ooligan@ooliganpress.pdx.edu
www.ooliganpress.pdx.edu

Library of Congress Cataloging-in-Publication Data is available by request.

Cover design by J. Adam Collins
Interior design by Poppy Milliken & Lorna Nakell

Contents

Publisher's Note		VII
Introduction		IX

VANCOUVER

City Introduction		015
A Cursed Poem	*Natasha Boskic*	019
A Lightness Dances	*Diane Tucker*	020
After the Tsunami	*Robin Susanto*	021
Alley Fragment and Name	*Christi Kramer*	022
Appleton	*Heather Haley*	023
At Wood-Edge Road	*George McWhirter*	024
Attempts to Know the Past	*Aislinn Hunter*	025
Aunt Jenny	*Alex Winstanley*	027
Beaches	*Andrea Bennett*	028
Beer, Blood & Bukowski	*Shannon Rayne*	029
Border Boogie (1969)	*Susan McCaslin*	030
Cabin Fever	*Anna Swanson*	034
Cars	*Carl Leggo*	036
Cell Phone	*Christopher Levenson*	037
Crows	*Sandy Shreve*	038
Desdemona (Durga)	*Joanne Arnott*	039
Everyday Things	*Lilija Valis*	040
Forgetting Mr. Low	*Bonnie Nish*	041
Ghostal or Vancouver's Geography of Loss	*Catherine Owen*	043
Hang On	*Marni Norwich*	044
Hollow	*David Zieroth*	047
Hummingbirds	*Bren Simmers*	048
In Event of Moon Disaster	*Lucia Misch*	049
Joy	*Kagan Goh*	050
Manning Park in the Dark	*Evelyn Lau*	052

Mount Pleasant	*Nikki Reimer*	055
Nadine	*Russell Thornton*	056
Offering	*Rita Wong*	057
Our Salt Spring Island Dinner	*Chris Gilpin*	058
Paris at Dusk	*Kim Fu*	059
Pelican	*Jason Sunder*	060
Power Saw Elegy	*Dennis E. Bolen*	061
Proust as Imperative	*Garry Thomas Morse*	062
Rushing Undergrowth	*Kate Braid*	064
Shrine for Every Part of You	*Jen Currin*	066
Song for the Dead	*Fran Bourassa*	067
Staring at the Window in the Private Family Visiting Cottage, William Head Penitentiary, April 2011	*Susan Musgrave*	069
Stealing Anatomies	*Elee Kraljii Gardiner*	070
Tai Chi, Van Dusen Gardens	*Trevor Carolan*	071
The Autopsy Report	*Catherine Owen*	073
The Goodnight Skirt	*Raoul Fernandes*	074
The Naming of Parts	*Kevin Spenst*	075
The Next Growing Season: a Glossary	*Renée Sarojini Saklikar*	077
The Stone	*Ibrahim Honjo*	078
The Wailing Machines	*Rob Taylor*	079
The Weight of Dew	*Daniela Elza*	080
The Wine Dark Sea	*Timothy Shay*	081
Tongue	*Susan Cormier*	083
What We Heard About the Canadians	*Rachel Rose*	084
Wordsong	*Heidi Greco*	085
You Go to Town	*Taryn Hubbard*	086
Story of the Pacific Poetry Project		091
Biographies		099
Attributions		109

PUBLISHER'S NOTE

Welcome to the Pacific Northwest's poetry community. You hold in your hands the inaugural publication of the Pacific Poetry Project, designed to capture this moment in poetry—the early years of the twenty-first century—from a region of North America unlike any other. We hope to bring you to the poetry salons, slams, and open-mic nights that are everywhere you look.

In the fall of 2009, a dedicated bunch of poetry lovers at Ooligan Press just happened to find themselves in the midst of a discussion about the state of poetry in our hometown—Portland, Oregon—and around the Pacific Northwest. What they came to discover was that poetry was happening all over the place in a grassroots way. Poetry represents a tiny slice of the revenue generated by the publishing industry. But as a visible and active community in our home, it is flourishing and bustling, full of life and energy. In Portland, Seattle, or Vancouver, you will find a poetry event happening weekly, if not nightly. These may be in our big bookstores, or they may be at a small wine bar, or they might even be in someone's living room, but it is a constant exchange among people who love the rhythm and meter of poetic work.

Based on this realization, Ooligan Press decided to develop an anthology of contemporary poetry from the Pacific Northwest. Very quickly, however, we realized that we were trying to do too much with one book. How could we possibly capture this buzzing, vibrant community between the covers of a single book? We couldn't. But we could launch a continuing project dedicated to two things: collecting and promoting the best poetic works from our region, and making those works available to a wider realm of readers.

Our first goal is relatively simple: we want to share the best of the best with our readers. Our second goal is a little more difficult, and slightly subversive (after all, we do live in Portland). In the last twenty or thirty years, poetry has become the provenance of a few smaller, dedicated non-profit publishers, like Copper Canyon, and of big university publishers, like the University of Pittsburgh Press (which both do amazing work). But even more, poetry seems to have become an outlier; something we used to appreciate and enjoy, but can't quite connect with now. Maybe this comes from having had to read the standard poetry fare in high school or college, which had little apparent connection to our teenage selves. Or maybe this comes from the lack of exposure and mainstream popularity of poetry, which is in part due to the fact that trade publishers don't see poetry as a financially viable product.

Whatever the cause, we think it's a shame. We think it is damaging to our cultural diversity and literary culture to be exposed to less poetry and fewer poets. Because, as Robert Duncan Gray writes in the Introduction to the book in your hands, "poetry is everywhere." So why not make poetry more "accessible"? Why not treat it like a rock star, as we do with other forms of writing? That is our goal with the Pacific Poetry Project. We want to bring poetry back to the mainstream conversation. We want to re-create the dynamic and vibrant poetry nights that happen among friends, but in the pages of these books (or on the screen of your favorite reading device). We want poetry to be for the people, as it always has been. We reject the notion that you have to "get" poetry to love it. We all get poetry. We just need to be given the permission to take whatever we do away from the reading or hearing of it. So for the publications with the Pacific Poetry Project logo on them, you are hereby given permission to think your own thoughts about the work inside. There's no right answer and there's no wrong answer. We want you to come to your own conclusions. But don't stop there. Take your thoughts and share them with a friend. Make poetry part of your conversation. Quote it on your favorite social network. Give it to your friends and family.

We are on a mission to bring poetry to the people. We need your help to do it. Enjoy *Alive at the Center* and welcome to the Pacific Poetry Project.

—*Ooligan Press*

ALIVE AT THE CENTER

(AN INTRODUCTION)

Everything is super. Super duper.
    Imagine Poetry (with a capital P) as a functional member of society.
Poetry gets a day job and earns a sizable paycheck. Poetry purchases
two luxury Mercedes Benzes and gives one to me—a brand new, shiny
Mercedes Benz! Super duper. The inside smells like lavender honey. I bake
Poetry a chocolate cake, by which I mean to say, Thank You. It doesn't turn
out perfect, but Poetry doesn't seem to care—so nonchalant!—Poetry
eats three big slices of my imperfect chocolate cake. Oh, all that chocolate
all over Poetry's face!
    Fantastic.
    Lately I have been thinking about poetry with a lowercase p, so
naturally I am worried. I have also been thinking about death, salt, and
hot water—or more specifically, deathsalt and hotwater. I have written a
mathematical equation:

$p = 4(hw) + (ds)$
Where p = poetry, h = hot, w = water, d = death and s = salt.

I have also written an accompanying recipe:
Poetry à la mode
    Combine four parts hotwater with one part deathsalt in a clean
        glass bowl.
    Stir vigorously with soft hands.
    Serve with ice cream.

A beekeeper friend of mine has a swarm up for grabs. I am worried
about the poetry of it. I guess I am worried about the poetry fading or
weakening in certain spots. What would we do for a poem compared
to what we would do for, say, a taco? And is there really all that much
difference between a poem and a taco?
    If all the poets of the world die, what then of poetry? What if all the
good poets died? Would good poetry be dead? Is poetry dependent on
poets? I don't think so, but really I don't know.
    I believe that poetry is not necessarily site-specific. You can find a
poem anywhere. You can find ten poems in bed, an entire volume inside
your kitchen—you certainly don't need to leave the house to write. There

is plenty of poetry all around. Poetry tucked in the sock drawer and under the couch. Poetry amongst the sharp knives. In the bathtub—hotwater. Deathsalt in the potatoes. Nothing is safe. That being said, go outside. It's nice outside.

I find a lot of poems at work, which is a bummer because I am at work. I find poems whilst riding my bicycle, which is also a bummer because I am riding my bicycle. It is often inconvenient to write a poem. Some poems must be ignored, or rather left alone—"ignored" seems harsh. Some poems remain free and that's super. Some poems are lost and some are eternally found. Whatever. Super duper. No big deal.

Sometimes I find poems perfect and easy. Poetry can be so easy. That's a big secret. Poets don't generally like to talk about it; perhaps we worry that such a declaration might lessen the value of our work. Truth be told, sometimes poetry is piss-easy and most of the time it carries no inherent value whatsoever. I come home from work and take all my clothes off in the kitchen. I say hello to the cat. I walk through the house to the bedroom and lie down. I get high and lost in the blades of the ceiling fan. I go to the bathroom and stare at myself in the mirror for a short while. Then I return to the bedroom, lie on the bed and the rest of the evening is all about poetry. I walk naked from room to room and find poems waiting for me. Eager poems rolling around. Belly-up poems. I hardly write, yet at the end of the night I have accumulated twenty poems or more! It must be some kind of magic.

Poetry is everywhere.

I once watched Ed Skoog recite poems in the middle of the night in an underground parking lot. I once watched Emily Kendal Frey recite poems on the third floor of a shopping mall. It happens in the weirdest places, under the most unlikely circumstances. Poetry seems to be all around, occupying the spaces in which we least expect to find it.

So here we are.

You hold in your hands a flock of poems. A gathering, yes. An organized pastiche poured fresh from the top left corner of America. American poetry is alive and well. American poetry is healthy. There is so damn much of it! How does this happen? A great many people share this huge experience, some sort of life in America, and feel the urge to report back. There are things here we feel must be shared, passed on. It is a beautiful thing. Super.

Upon reading this collection, one cannot help but feel a great sense of relief. Everything is super. Poetry is fat and fun and full of beauty. Super duper. The problems we face today are bigger and more complicated than those we faced yesterday, but rest assured—there is poetry in between, around and inside everything, and every day we are getting better and better at exposing it. Everything is going to be just fine.

I have written a recipe for this book.

Alive at the Center
Combine four parts hotwater, one part deathsalt, a dash of fresh ginger, a clove of crushed garlic, five pickled pigs feet, one sea anemone, three tusks, two bundles of cashmere, a pint of Puget Sound, a rumble of kitten purr, a chorus of traffic jam, two pocketfuls of lavender honey, a whalebone of satisfied hunger and two feet of sadness, a lungfull of unmelodious childsong, a mile of rusted train track, a never ending ambulance siren, two slices of cold cheese pizza, raw beef on the edge, fresh hoof, warm blood of beet, nine bridges, a dash of Douglas Fir, a waterfall of black coffee and one day-old donut. Salt and pepper to taste. Stir vigorously with soft hands. Serve with ice cream and imperfect chocolate cake.

Everything is super.

—Robert Duncan Gray

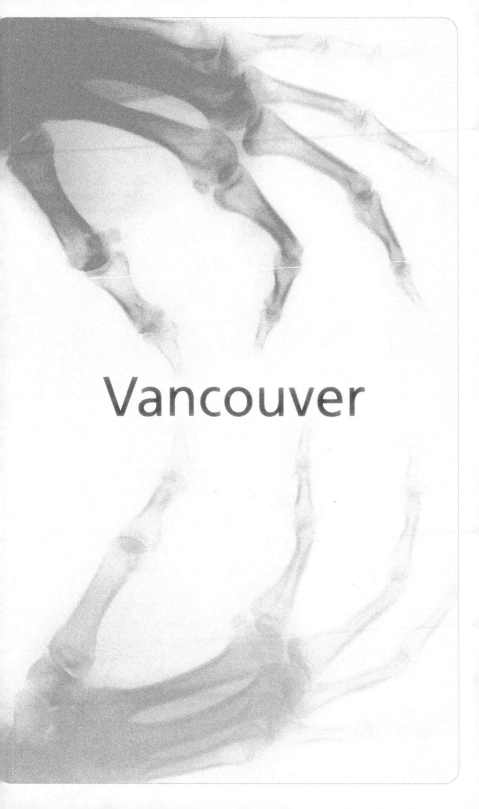

Vancouver

POEMS FROM VANCOUVER, BRITISH COLUMBIA

One thing has been clear from the start: to attempt to represent the poetry voices in Vancouver—present and future—is a bold undertaking, if not an impossible one. We will not be presumptuous about the future or claim that we have entirely covered the present. What we can claim is to have presented a mere taste of Vancouver's richness in poetry.

One vital aspect of an anthology for me is the possibility for a gathering—the opportunity to create a community. As editors, we wanted to offer a selection that crossed over, through, and into different poetic sensibilities by way of established poets, new poets, work published and unpublished, and a diversity of themes.

I want to extend my sincere gratitude to Bonnie Nish and Robin Susanto for accompanying me through the challenges and joys of this adventure.

The three of us invited 125 poets to mark Vancouver's 125th anniversary. We focused on poets whose voices we had heard in libraries, cafés, on the streets, in reading series, at festivals… These included poets who work hard at organizing and supporting spaces in which poetry can be heard. We asked around for recommendations, for representatives of different communities, for names we could not afford to miss. We were interested in including people who represent different schools, trends, and blends. In the meantime, I was reading poetry book after poetry book and requesting poems.

Midway through, there was a postal strike, which added an unexpected twist to the process. We requested both electronic and paper submissions to make sure that at least one of them reached us. (Our sincere apologies if some work never made it.)

If I had to sum up the approach, I would call it *poetic*. We put some constraints in place and stayed open to what showed up. We appreciated convergence and serendipity. All three editors had to agree on the poems selected. We were pleased to discover the overlap between us, and where there wasn't agreement we had to pull out the "convince me" card. We made very few compromises and tried to keep politics out of this harvest. One thing is for sure: most of the poems we've brought to you have been spoken into the Vancouver air and know its seasons.

We debated at length if we, the editors, should submit poems. We decided against it, but then I began to feel that it would be unfair not to show up for the gathering. And if I was going to show up, then I did not want the other two editors excluded. It boiled down to an "all or nothing" decision. We were in this together, along with Vancouver's poets.

We hope the value here is not simply in offering you a sampling of poets' work, but in offering a chance to become more acquainted, more related, to a bigger community. This anthology gives us the added benefit of expanding this community across three cities. Mix, mingle, enjoy.

Kind Regards

— Daniela Elza

A CURSED POEM

I
If you leave me
I'll put a curse on you:

I'll embed my eyes,
under your ribs
to wake you at night
and look through you;

I'll glue my skin
on your fingertips
not to touch a thing
without feeling me.

I'll nail my scent into every
Spring petal,
when you smell a flower,
my scent to stab you.

II
If I leave you,
because of a look
because of a word or two,
because of a subtle quiver
because of the time
that drips down the window,
because of the tender rapture.

Blind, I will walk on Earth;
It will rain endlessly,
I will drown   unaware.

A LIGHTNESS DANCES

a lightness dances
a tangle of wet hair gathers
momentum; she cries
look mama, here's my cartwheel!
her limbs blur
whir in a gymnastic mist
and with a soft thump
resolve against the grass

splayed on the ground she laughs
and sighs, a snowless angel
my heavenless angel
I laugh and cry to see her
at night when she curls
suddenly long arms and legs
in futile fetal pose

because she's already born
we're all squeezed into daylight
against our will
together we squint at the sun
take baby steps
hold hands

she holds out her arms
begs I take her back in time
the sun keeps rising
suspended like a pendulum
counting our hours down

Diane Tucker

AFTER THE TSUNAMI

The sea is all wrong
Its surging sullen, its shimmer thick as pitch
Its waves stammer as they crash
Headfirst with the crack of bones
Whole coasts swept with splinters of syllables
Whole islands told without a tongue

The wind spoke, instead of breeze
The hundred thousand names that no longer belong
Names that are called, names that don't answer

But still you touch your lips to the sea
Run your hand over the water, as if it was the fur of a sleeping animal
To whisper to the sea the houses and the vegetable gardens
The fisher folks, and the tourists who came to sleep softly on the sand
The little children who held on briefly before closing their eyes
The hundred thousand names,
Names that are whispered, names that are released

(And I have seen the whole world whispering with you
Lining whole continents with lit candles
Emptying its pockets into the sea)

Now you who belong to the sea must lull the sea to sleep
Lull the sea to sleep

ALLEY FRAGMENT AND NAME

Pull a fortune from the alley; card of wisdom reversed or blessed

Corrugated cardboard alley (say painted red)

A river of alley: where window of light, window shades drawn
Slick spill of pollen and milk
And this is neighborhood drawn by alley

Someone wrote a message, rolled it, slid it inside a bottle, sealed it, tossed
it into the
alley…

So winds and current might lift it away.

Shadow alley — wild electric sizzle — touch with the eye alley

Peel back the walls of the house; exposed beam, night sky, negative space
Touch alley of bolt and screw; touch steel, acrylic, orange

Dance in the alley, why not? Head touch the ground. Broken alley pours
out light.

Here in the narrow of grate and pail; corner of copper patched over

Pipe of echo; aluminum; hollow to sky alley; darker pallet of rain
(Do you remember where you placed this dab of yellow?)
Spackle alley, rubbed smooth, made rough. Pull fingers free from gloves,
touch

Uncork the message, run nail along wax, waft of whisky and whimsy,
crack

Perhaps it is a love letter to alley. Perhaps answer to our prayer.

What is endless

This room is alley. So is your heart

Christi Kramer

APPLETON

Hookah squats on carpet, Buddha-
esque. Undulating spirals of sapphire
smoke hula up her nose. That buzz.
That buzz that slows your blood,

calls you back to bed like a lover.
Soothes your inner asshole.
BC bud. Best bud
in the world. Worth risking jail for.

High-resolution satellite images.
Narcs' warrant executed Tuesday.
Grow-op raided Wednesday.
Dozens of firearms. Five thousand plants.

Big bust for a small town, says Constable Cook.
For export, for sure. Cultivation facilities dismantled.
Straight people relieved. Green party over,
but Zoe cried. It was the best job ever!

Dope dealers pay well. Her boyfriend
sold product at school. Their responsibilities
included digging a tunnel under the border,
blaming black fingernails and muddy jeans
on dirt biking at the gravel pit.

Parents were shocked. We thought she was
on Facebook, chatting. We thought he was
on the Internet, with her, boy's father chiding,
it's APPLE ton, son, not Marijuanaton!

AT WOOD-EDGE ROAD

The city seems too green
to be inhabited by death.

One expects blood immediately
to grow into the trunk and branches of red
alder, to find the nova of its spiral galaxy,
its clotted pods of crushed crimson, exploded
in the victim's head, laid daintily,
face-down on the asphalt. A posy of mini
daffodils under a tree, nearby — this troop of yellow-haired
girl guides, set to lead across the black lea
of the road, stops, in order not to disturb
the least detail in the yellow-jacketed,
taped and labelled crime scene — curbed,
their own glorious colour, perplexed
by the awful similarity.

George McWhirter

ATTEMPTS TO KNOW THE PAST

I do not want to say *darkness* or *door*,
or *the dark door we walk in through.*
This is no way to understand the past.
Will write instead of those regions on maps
coloured in by the imagination. Or the dusk
that is the backdrop of the universe —
how, when I was a child, I pictured space
hanging like a painting on a huge white canvas
inside a gilded frame. Infinity a notion that could
send a person over the edge, as in those Sinbad films
where whole ships careen over earth's steep curb,
and men gallop past the known periphery,
flogging their animals into the sea.

I will not write of the absence of light,
God's holy show, ripe orchards tilting their fruit
to the heavens. Or of the sun tossed like a gold coin
into the bucket of the sky. Instead I'll praise
what I have before me: a book, a lamp,
a chair beside the open window, a pocket watch
whose hour is caught in the glass eye of the moon.
The thread of history as dun-coloured
as a corridor in a painting by Vermeer.
Knock once on a Street in Delft, watch a woman
asleep at her table, look through the slant
entrance to the room beyond. All these portals.
Apertures that could take us anywhere.

The womb a door. The past a door. There,
I've said it. The future a bright yellow bird
in the corner of the room, singing. How easily
we fall off the map, sail into new worlds distracted
by song. Once, I stood in the National Museum lost
for hours in the radiant sheenof a pearl earring.
Terrible monsters here, they said, of those realms
where anything could happen, where anything

did happen. Who was I yesterday? The day before?
How have the rooms of the past remembered me,
if they remember me at all? Open a door onto the pitch
of space, onto the sunless caves we came from.
What sadness there, what hope, what delirium.

Aislinn Hunter

AUNT JENNY

A fallen bridge
in your eyes,
and on the far side
the lilies of lucidity.

Satan called you out
into the garments of death —
convinced you
to swallow those pills.

And you lay dying
in your room for two days,
slipping into dreams,
as cool green water
trickled over your skin;

you were prom queen,
a princess of sunflowers
in your youth.

But then you were Ophelia.

That awkward word,
the diagnosis
stretches between us like green rope, or
a fallen bridge.
And on the far side —
lilies. And I cry
for the broken stem
of your mind.

BEACHES

She and I talk about home like it's the first pair of underwear
you picked out for yourself. Didn't pinch; developed holes; etc. Home
is the first place you live without your parents, we decide, because
we are like that.

Her boyfriend is mop-headed, grins like a kid with a bucket and
spade. Sometimes she's the beach and sometimes she's the mom, saying
Sunscreen, fer chrissakes, sunscreen. I prefer to say partner, have
also heard sweetheart. I dunno, yet, if I have a partner or a
sweetheart or what. You've stuck your legs out one side of the
umbrella, she says, and stayed mostly in the shade. She cracks a joke
about fish aplenty.

What we are going to do with our lives: work with our hands? The
way people who think about home as underwear work with their hands.
The way they always go home. And what of our loves? Well, we'll write
poetry the way fishmongers write poetry, knifing a steelhead open like
a cherished book.

Andrea Bennett

BEER, BLOOD & BUKOWSKI

We didn't quite know it at the time
but we were making art—
the night we got kicked out of three bars
chasing ghosts across Vancouver.

You were heartbroken, drunk on whisky
I was heartbroken, intoxicated by anger.

We raised fists to the shadow of a smug moon
before downing a pint toasting our misfortune.

No one wants a lonely drunk, you shouted
somewhere between Water & Carrel Street.

You had your nose broken
when you hit on the tattooed bartender
busted your lip wide open

when you started rambling
something about the masquerade of the Haida Indian
and the desperation in Bukowski's poetry.

I fell off my bar stool laughing
when you mixed up the two images.

That night, stumbling back to East Van
dripping with beer and blood
we were a walking Pollock painting
giggling all the way home
wondering why no one was offended
over Bukowski.

BORDER BOOGIE (1969)

You who go out on schedule
to kill, do you know
there are eyes that watch you?
—Denise Levertov

1

Moon-pent in a white vw,
heading up the freeway north from Seattle,
sperm-like rain snaking up the windshield
toward Nirvana, British Columbia,

I am twenty-two
and deathless.

My boyfriend Tim and I slip
across the border just after Blaine
where he blew his mind on acid
a month ago on our first reconnaissance
of the route, hip, cool, tuned
to Coltrane's A Love Supreme.

2

The horrors of Hanoi,
napalm stuck in our skulls,
Levertov's logged words
encoding my journal.

Simon Fraser's radical curriculum
promises manna for the disenchanted,
tales of students storming the faculty lounge,
"Be in's" for beleaguered flowering ones.

Tim drags along, averse to academics,
burying his letter from the draft board
deep in his duffle bag, moving
breathless past customs officials.

Susan McCaslin

3
His dad chose for him a military career.
He told me how in officers' training
he leapt from a helicopter,
shot and skinned a rabbit, vomited,
then heaved himself out of there,

"tuned in, turned on, dropped out,"
found Monty his guru, and
a macrobiotic regime till I
caught him munching an O Henry.

Returning from a seminar on Blake
and the mythopoetic mind, I
became "The Little Girl Lost"
who found her lion deep

into Cream and Miles,
sprawled on the orange shag rug,
headphones riveted to his ears,
an astronaut trolling inner space,

splayed like Da Vinci's man,
skinny, open-faced.

4
He graduated (barely) in physics
but sought the Tao of imagination,

did piecework, house painting,
lineman jobs, stoned, toked up,

and with his first cheque bought me
a shimmering shift of red-orange glitter,
Aphrodite dress from a head shop.

He followed me to Vancouver,
pining for home, yet home meant

the draft and Vietnam,
hot killing fields and hollowed eyes.

5
Up all night typing papers on Poe's Berenice,
and Ligeia, I take to sporting dark capes,
grow pale with anemia,
believe that in another incarnation
I had been Poe's child wife Virginia Clemm.
(I always become what I research.)

My thesis grows pregnant with itself,
swells to 300 pages, mysterious,
white, like Moby Dick.

Tim, restless, disenchanted,
drives back and forth to Seattle.
We who had considered marriage,

split. I touch his head one last time
and choose to stay in Canada:
first hostel, hotel,
and finally, home.

6
Stuck with unknowing
all these years, I wonder:

Did he get snared by the draft?
Did he break and bleed in Southeast Asia?
Is his name inscribed on the wall in Washington?

Or is he a banker now,
easing into late mid-life
with a wife, a dog, and grandchildren on the way?

Googling gives no leads.
But who really needs to know?
The slide of sex, the glimmer gone,

all seems impossible, improbable
to my 60-something life.

Susan McCaslin

Nevertheless, I would offer
more than ironies:
this last image of him falling
downstairs in a pool of his own light.

Errant knight,
held in a poem's peace.

CABIN FEVER

If I had a bottle of wine up here, I'd hold the neck in my fist and tip it up too fast. Let the weight of it rip through the long dusty day right to my feet. Like rain. Or a road. Or somewhere to go.

If I had a bottle of wine, I'd lie on the ground and practise at happy drunk. Despite a hundred feet of good ladder and the thrill of distance in the dark. Or that place under the hatch where the ladder cage opens to the sky and you lean back, harnessless, into it. Because you can't climb with a bottle in your hand, I'd say. Knowing a thousand famous men have proven me wrong.

Or I'd sit here and love this place like they would. All the good trees. Fireweed tender as a second chance, not knowing what came before. The things men tell each other when they're drunk. How conversation, even love, becomes a ladder, and they climb anything that goes up.

Hammock, I'd think. Sky. Runaway sun. I could eat corn and run open-mouthed and greasy into the woods where the sun went. Maybe it's simple as a picnic table with a pot of boiling corn. Easy as forgetting my fear of the strangers who roll up my driveway at dusk. Waving them closer with butter on my hands, grease stains on my pants where I wipe off my palms. Corn, I'd say, kernels filling my mouth. A mouth full of perfect days. The butter ground down to the bottom of its thin metal wrapper. The endless shucking of corn.

I could love this place right. Serve up summer night like fall-apart home-made dessert. But before I do, I find Al Purdy's already chewed it up and spat it out perfect, and I hate him for it. Running and running naked with summer in your mouth. Fuck you, Al Purdy. I run my teeth over the kernels of all my favourites. Wanting to see them suffer. But no. They do that already. So beautifully.

It seems they are always drinking. Or undoing the drinking of their past. The hard glamour of damage. Polished like infidelity, like leaving. Why try? I think. When they've already been here so much better and drunker and more foolish with love.

I turn to offer them more corn, but they're gone. Have thrown their husks on the grass and called it beautiful. Even laughter is a ladder. Have left their garbage and taken my truck. Are drinking my wine a bottle each like beer. Are looking for another roadside stand. Hey, I yell, but it's twenty cents a cob and six for a buck. It's summer. It's corn. It's so fucking cheap. They hold a twenty out the window and watch it flap. Six for a dollar. One good hot night. Somewhere to go. Corn. Corn so sweet you eat it raw. Windows cranked. Gasoline. That perfect speed that comes with its own warm wind.

CARS

cars drift down
sw Marine Drive

a long prose sentence
on Valium

the beginning forgets
all syntactical energies

the amnesiac sentence
refuses the period's finality

in this senseless sentence
with no beginning or end

some cars pull while others push
no train of linear thought

a sentence can be stepped
into only once, never again

lines on a map, lines in a story
a long breath that might last

Carl Leggo

CELL PHONE

Once only important people like pilots
or battery commanders needed to know
everything as it happened, but now, like a medical intern
I too am on call twenty-fours a day
with no data too trivial not to warrant an interruption:
at the opera its urgent beep disturbs
Pavarotti's "Nessun Dorma" How could anyone sleep?
Its trill protests halfway through
the memorial service at the cenotaph.
Like a concealed weapon or a portable Buddha,
it goes with me everywhere, stakes a claim on me,
when I am "eating or opening a window or just walking dully along."
And when I answer I am always aware
of being overheard. Privacy? I *want* even strangers to know
the important deals I make, the assignations.
And anyway this amulet protects me
against surprises, like now that ten-ton truck
that abruptly appears from the right in mid-sentence
while I'm travelling at eighty through a red light
and frames my last…

CROWS

'Cras' (Latin) means 'tomorrow.'

Out of all four corners of the world,
these ancients with tomorrow on their tongues
gather one by one,

cackle from whatever throne
they find to occupy—
at the edges of our eyes, the crows'

feet etch our every smile,
as if the only thing in life that matters
is our laughter.

Creatures of both earth and sky, they do not
care if we believe them evil,
dread them as death's messengers

or simply scorn them for the mess they make
scavenging through garbage in the park.
Always dressed for funerals,

crows know they are the pallbearers for our souls,
their gift, to find the glitter in what we leave behind.

Sandy Shreve

DESDEMONA (DURGA)

he came at me in a fierce rage
i felt a small crack open in my
forehead, Kali
burst forth and struck him
a fierce blow
and he was felled
Kali continued
moving about the scene
devouring men high and low
and then
i said, *stop*
not the shaper
her eyes strayed toward Emilia
and again
i said, *stop*
with the place now cleared
but for the four left standing
Kali returned to slip inside
my head
i went to the cupboard
for rags and salt
i opened the closet
for the mop and bucket
started running cold water

no idea what Iago or Emilia
will do with themselves, but
a woman needs to keep her
attention on what she herself
needs to do: every good bloodbath
must be followed by a scrub and rinse,
a home is not a battlefield after all

EVERYDAY THINGS

If everything is sacred
you will use the knife carefully.

The meal you will place on the table
will nourish more than the body.

The vow you take to serve
will turn sacrifice to pleasure.

If all things carry meaning
you will let pain heal.

No matter if your home is one room
you will place a flower to greet the light.

If blessings often come disguised, you
will take home the thin dog with the sad eyes.

Lilija Valis

FORGETTING MR. LOW

Downtown on the Eastside
where diners close late
with metal bars
strapped up against the flat belly of a doorway,
rumours spread faster than rolling paper
between junkies and pushers.
It's Saturday morning, early, three am.
Vans begin to roam the streets
looking for good drugs, bad girls
and Mr. Low sits in his corner, undisturbed
as a buzz begins to stir in an already buzzing street life.
Pimps scream up and down the road
ready to jump on encroaching vendors
while their girls smoke cigarettes in bunches,
hunched under a street light
with skirts hiked up almost to their pelvic bones,
night air slips under to remind them business is slow,
the long fingers of hunger
stretch across their thinning young bodies
pushed to the limit of uncaring.

Mr. Low shifts position
lifts his eyes down the street
where a tomb has formed in the alleyway.
Boys pounding boys into the pavement
screams in the night,
the sound of an empty bed,
a mother's terror,
wakes her miles away.
Mr. Low listens,
shuts his eyes and remembers,
there were times when women touched him,
boys followed him,
now he sits as drool drips down his double chin
into his soaking lap.
A siren startles him, someone pokes him.
"Hey old man! Go home."
Mr. Low nods, they move on.
He waits for the smell of coffee

from across the street to permeate the air,
until then he sits comfortably watching, undisturbed.

The buzz is quietening to a dim hustle
the hookers have all been picked up,
their pimps sleep on cots
in the cramped boarded rooms
of a burnt out building.
The boys have bandaged their cuts
and gone home to mother
while the morning dew settles
on Mr. Low's shoes
and he knows he is forgotten,
just as he forgets.

Bonnie Nish

GHOSTAL OR VANCOUVER'S GEOGRAPHY OF LOSS

Beyond the Ovaltine, before Save On Meats, O, I have closed myself
to this, the shopping carts heavy with cardboard, rigs, clothing, bi-
cycle parts,
people alien because, I know this now too much, drugs have abducted
them until
there is only, what I saw you become, a hunger and I have stopped wanting
to give. As I pass fast and blind through the homeless, their transac-
tions with
dealers a dance, a man, not you but still it could have been, careens to-
wards me,
overcoat, hoodie, arms extended in leftover desire,
"Honey, where you been all my life, you're so beautiful," he says, knowing
I will ignore him, what else can I do, stirred by how long it takes to kill
longing, and yet, not wanting to be touched, ever again, your ghost
down here,
might have been you, how can I forgive this, grey day, boarded-up buildings,
you dead and I no longer able to feel for the lost of the earth, wanting
to breathe
immune for a while in the pure and shining lie of you not gone, us
with plans,
the man with outstretched arms clean, embraced by loved ones, not passed
by cold on the pavement between Save On Meats, the Ovaltine.

HANG ON

The bus driver says
"hang on,"
and I want to say,
sir, I am hanging on
as best I can:
to the post,
to my head,
to my partner,
to the Earth.
But my life is falling through
my fingers
like fine white sand,
and this grasping—
well, we all know
the thing we grasp at
eludes us
all the more.
You implore us to
hang on, and sir, I
know you mean well,
but I think in all fairness
we require more
explicit instruction.

"Hang on to
the thought that birthed us,
to the fullness of our hearts,
to the present love that
fuels each moment.
Hang on to the Light,
to the wisdom of the ages,
to the spirit that rushes
through your pen,
to the calm beneath the pain,
to the fast-flowing river
that underlies all sorrow.
Hang on to your faith in
the ever-changingness of everything,
in goodness,

Marni Norwich

and white, wild-growing freesia."
And you, too, sir,
you must hang on
for all of us:
to your belief in
the power of the road
to deliver us to
our destinies;
to your commitment to this route and
the work of ferrying your
fellow-travelers
from place to place.
Perhaps the key is
for all of us to hang on,
but loosely.
Maybe with an
open stance and
relaxed arms we can better
flow with the bumps and
sudden stops along
this winding roadway.
And it does wind, sir,
and even you,
who drive it every day,
must be jarred
from time to time
by the unpredictable actions of
people and machines.

Sir, my stop has come,
and I bid you a
good evening,
wishing only that
you may grip
loosely to the
road, which bends and
sways like a tree limb
in the breeze,
but tightly to
hope,
for yourself and
for us all,

your passengers on this
sacred vessel,
this ambling
gliding
careening
living
dream.

Marni Norwich

HOLLOW

Suddenly I am hollowed out, at the lip
of weeping, panic in my throat, because
        the season changes, and into the pause
        between the shifting moments slips
a blankness unprepared for, and someone's
leaving, and all my plans come undone.

Nor does it help that the dark
falls early, the clouds blocking light
        so even a pleasant walk cannot ignite
        inside me the necessary spark
of hopefulness that gives a shape to each hour
that fights off what comes to devour

the little I've now become: alone
to make the day, routine not yet kicked in.
        I kick the sidewalk trash while within
        whirls my own lean cyclone
sucking from me what once I was: one whose joy
at living and arriving was not so easy to destroy.

HUMMINGBIRDS

Jacked up on sugar, they zip-line
over teens in jean cutoffs
whose hands brush, interlock.

As they scout the park's perimeter
for a secluded nook, territorial males show off,
ascend thirty feet in a surge of hormones

only to free fall: a rufous blur.
Whirligigs in a gale wind, hearts
displayed in their bright throats.

Spring stoppered in a bird
no bigger than your thumb—
the urge to screw around

in the back of a car, forget
who you are, put beak to
stamen, drink it all.

Bren Simmers

IN EVENT OF MOON DISASTER

*In the summer of 1969, William Safire wrote the address
Nixon would give the nation if Neil Armstrong and Edwin
Aldrin became stranded on the lunar surface with no hope of
rescue. It was entitled "In Event Of Moon Disaster."*

In event of moon disaster,
do not think
that we have put men
in robot bodies without reason

That perhaps the eleven layer A7L spacesuit
is padded casket comfortable
Instead,
remember that those careful white costumes
are the smallest Eden
we have ever put an Adam inside of

Do not think of weightless suffocation

Think instead of your children
with their heads under their desks
of the smell of coffee
burning your re-entry into the kitchen
the initials pocket knifed into the bus window
the footprints in steady dust

Do not feel weighted by the lead clothes you wear
in case the bomb drops.
   They are not as heavy as you think

JOY

I was at a house party celebrating Canada Day
when I met a woman named Joy.
I said: "It's a joy to meet you Joy."
She beamed at me,
then said: "I am manic depressive."
At once the conversation dried up.
Not knowing what to say
made an excuse
I had to call my girlfriend.
A lie.
I avoided her staying upstairs
while she waited lost in the party below.
She reminded me of a dog I once had.
Aalways happy to see me,
jumping and licking my face,
overwhelmed by its affection,
I fled upstairs, afraid to come down.
Eventually my mother lost her patience:
"OK, we'll give him away to the S.P.C.A."
She made me accompany her.
I carried the dog in my arms.
It looked at me with the saddest eyes,
wavering on the brink of tears.
He spoke to me:
"Don't leave me."
I swear I did not imagine it.
By the time we arrived at the S.P.C.A.,
I said: "Mum I change my mind
I want to keep him."
"No. After all the trouble
you've caused me,
dragging me all the way here,
you don't deserve a dog."

Kagan Goh

I am sorry Joy.
I was afraid.
I didn't understand
until I too was diagnosed manic-depressive
eight years ago on Valentine's Day of all days.
This is the way I feel every time
I am led back to the psych ward,
an obedient dog
crying to God, don't leave me.

MANNING PARK IN THE DARK

The night we came through the storm
and survived, I loved my life for the first time.
The world was white, there were no other cars
on the winding highway to light our way
as we climbed the summit of the mountain pass,
anchored by instinct to the vanishing road.
We were alone on our approach
to Summerland, roped to life
by a single strand of breath—
I breathed in and out
as we sped around curve after curve
in the blindness, the road gone under our feet
but for the slick of tires sticking to snow,
the guiding lines invisible,
white paint under white flurry.
The screen of the windshield blazed
our sight with filaments of bright,
snow whipping horizontal towards us
like a million stars from the universe.
Then I was calm. I let go.
I could have fallen forward forever,
the air tasting like honey,
stillness opening at the centre of my body,
I wanted it to go on forever.
Breath, silence, piano music
faintly stirring from the CD player,
strings guiding us down into a valley
pillowed in fog, lights twinkling
in the small towns. Then the arc of a flashlight
through the air, the animal
lying across the road in a heap
of flesh as if asleep,
the screeching swerve back into our lives.

Evelyn Lau

MEH'S ON CBC!

whod'a thought this worn paper immigrant
would be on canada's national radio its voice and thought

(used to think CBC was what made you canadian
'cause authentic canadians seemed to be always saying
'did you hear the CBC yesterday' 'last nite on CBC'
but there was something wrong with us 'cause we'd rather listen
    to 50's doo-wop and motown on the goldie oldies station
    I admit there was a time I tried to listen but my ears would
        slip lips and so would time mime a part-time canadian
        no I'm not connected to the country no ear to the ground-
-ing nation the catsup chip state of mainly unity)

meh is so proud at last she's being noticed
'so the secrets of your shan cooking is out'
people'd said words dashed with her own exclamations
secrets are watched out!

during the interview she puts on her best english
handles it like pro unlike the minced languages she normally uses
chopping thai shan and english other accents picked up second-hand
she explains things as I'd never heard her explain to me
and though I turn away from the microphone I can't help staying to
    overhear

(later she asks me, 'did you hear my story?'
as if telling the reporter was a way of telling me
and I admit the stuff I hear is stuff for keeps)

every once in a while standing before the stove
stirring chicken curry and frying slices of golden *topu*
she can't help it, her hand automatically reaches up flicks on the exhaust fan
even though the noise is overwhelming and annoys the reporter
she's worried about the house stinking up smell a sensitive thing
but for the most part she concedes to the reporter and turns it off

'tell me' says the reporter, 'what do you think about when you smell these
    foods?'
and meh who's never been asked that kind of question
but who likes to humor the game anyway
answers
'that I'm hungry.'

MOUNT PLEASANT

under the weather or above the fault lines, there has been no measurable change in our mental health. we brace for "the big one," whatever that means. blush of pink blooms against the landscape. we could chart our progress against tectonic plates and topographical maps but common sense would dictate we limit such questionable use of our already limited resources. which is to say, hand me an upper. what small philosophical forces are gathering momentum behind the counters of this city's bakeries and in languages unfamiliar to our ears? we have grown fat in recent months and unprepared for evacuation. pink buds on branches and blouses. we engage in commerce and call it action. which is to say, i bought a sweater and ate a cookie. alone and isolated in the basement suites of the lower east side, we ponder our day jobs and indulge ourselves in the existential crises du jour. imagine to reach some lofty heights, as if we were on the second floor, as if we were Baudelaire. surely Foucault never drank so much coffee in one sitting, and Virginia Woolf wrote in spite of, and not because of, her depression. you might argue that one good Stein deserves another but i am tired and i have been kicked out of every cafe on Main Street for crimes against the artist-run collective. no, you can't use the bathroom, i just washed the floor. this hourglass is impatient and catches up with us. we are too easily distracted by the fashions of the time. when we return to the car it is covered with cherry blossoms. an innocuous landscape amidst the rush of cars. is that a hooker? such detritus, this daily existence. a little room, a beast to scratch, and a warm body to lean up against. how can we measure our progress against the inimitable forces of consumerism in the distance? we haven't shaved in weeks. and guilt, that useless emotion, chafes. somewhere a raccoon clambers up a wire fence with an evil glint in his eye. still the blossoms fall and we use them to wipe the tears off each other's faces.

NADINE

Night of quick, wild rain, gusts off the inlet. Blackness
lit only by glintings of rain, bored through to nothing
by my car headlights. I stood waiting on the pier.
She stepped out of the blackness and into dim sheen
and faced me, saying nothing yet gesturing. At first,
I thought that she didn't speak English. Then her friend
was there beside her, down from an unseeable ship.
The three of us piled into my taxi. I apologized
for not realizing that she couldn't speak or hear.
The two of them in the back seat, the friend giggled,
chattered half to himself, while she sat forward, leaned
to the side and looked out at me from where
she was never to be woven into the sound of a voice
and where she seemed hidden, even when she displayed
her widest smile, her hand on my shoulder, touching at me
to turn, turn left, turn, turn right — knowing I knew the way,
and at every instant teasing, flirting. Then the laughter
in her eye-flash in the rearview mirror undid me,
the clamped-down face with which I peddled myself
trip by trip fell away. We were together, the three of us,
the wind at the black glass around us the breath
of a childlike presence welcoming us further, further,
the rain on the roof the tapping of a heart. They taught me
how to sign *no problem, friend and asshole.*
They were Similkameen, they were my age,
and had been in Vancouver a month. They had gotten
an American twenty-dollar bill for the taxi fare
from the ship to their hotel and back again. They gave me
all of it, refusing the change, the money adding up
to more than a decent tip. The friend, the girl's cousin,
her sarcastic, playful, hilarious pimp, told me
the sailors had made fun of her, and neither of them
stood for that. Anyhow, the sailors sent her back. *Get us somebody else,*
they said. *We want a talking whore.*

OFFERING

faith hides in little pockets like the heart
& the throat. born with a serious streak
the width of an altar, i climb the stairs in
that first home, the zhi ma wu, black
sesame childhood sweet, squeeze soya
beans in a rough white cotton bag, hold
my mother's workworn hands. what do
any of these small gestures mean
except that they have carried me
into now? shadows in the corner.
dust on the shelves & in the blood. an
archival endeavour, let the fragments
stand together, make us larger than the
sum of the individuals. float from
quote to quote, to shore the body of
a man with hairy legs, a mi'kmaq
woman with dark hair who curls into
the sheets like a child, a gay boy who
made the best damn bannock i've ever
tasted. there's no justice for him to die.
ground to push against: red earth,
bloody earth, stolen earth. what the pen
takes, the throat can return.

OUR SALT SPRING ISLAND DINNER

We invited the first and last words in postmodernism to our rebuttal, our Salt Spring Island dinner.

We cooked and served, they had to move their mouths fast to keep up. Foucault attacked discursive formations in the garlic mashed potatoes with his fork. Kristeva admitted the roasted carrots were too tender to be construed as phallocentric. Baudrillard crumbled up hyperreal simulacra and sprinkled it over his kale. Pass the bricolage, Barthes said.

Cumin and turmeric legends floated through the lamb curry, hinting at exotic intertextuality, a flaw in our argument perhaps. Fortunately, by that point, the blackberry wine had soaked Lacan's semiotics, making each morsel derivative of nothing but itself.

Everyone's body of work digested the reproof in the pudding differently. Derrida deconstructed himself in giggle fits. Barthes sung the song of the Swedish meta-chef. Saussure and Heidegger tried to do the dishes, but ended up running their foam-covered fingers through each other's moustaches.

Afterward, in the old orchard, we exhaled our education. Even the spiders spinning geometry could snare none of last century's fashionable nonsense as it exited our bodies in a puff of ganja, and vanished into the intelligent night. Our feline sentinel assumed her perch in the plum tree, on guard against any who would argue the full moon is not a perfect circle.

Chris Gilpin

PARIS AT DUSK

Sunsets gather in a room
the size of an elevator,
waiting for their audition.
They parade past, one by one,
wearing red zebra-print dresses,
hats with iridescent feathers,
pink leg warmers that bunch
unflatteringly around the calf.
They sing in high, warbling voices,
overact, all daggers and tears,
do that same vanishing act,
hoping the director hasn't been dulled
to just another pretty face.

> You bit a crepe hot from my hand
> on a sidewalk narrow as a bicycle.
> We fell into patio chairs
> that belonged to no one,
> held hands. On the wind,
> veal bones stewed to melt, cigars,
> butter like solace. The smooth oval
> of the fountain pool rippled in dialogue
> with our faces, then spread over the city,
> painting all the buildings
> the colour of a bruised plum.

Our sunset stood on stage
and made predictable choices:
monologue from Shakespeare,
lovers by a fountain in Paris.
Songbirds burst from her mouth,
cleaved the spotlight into *long purples,*
her clothes spread wide.
Then we remembered
why the bard is The Bard,
why we weep for Ophelia,
why the heart still shocks at the sky.

PELICAN

Ax in Greek, your bill would
bully wood. Dipped wingtip
to coast oceans that swallow miles
of oil & feathers. Maybe you
slipped under a shadow
pouch bulbous with whispers
that cut the air into crayfish.
Your cry pushes
a tugboat full of crustaceans
to boiling. How you love
to eat them! Was Mexico
a misplaced handshake
after God forgot to wash
the black out of blue
a distracted murmur at
the podium? Now nod
& vuln yourself raw before
the Eucharist, your blood
a forgotten promise, your
bill-pressed chest
a question mark.

Jason Sunder

POWER SAW ELEGY

Sandpaper time
Mill planed tree
Smelted ore
Pipelined fluids of the ground

Teenage workers of the world
Frolic in the affluent effluence
Drive mighty travel machines
To revel hard amid the distractions of growth

That drug be too strong
That car be too fast
That might be too many beers
To drink
To drive through a grove

Moloch trunk cathedral
Bearing crush
Cerebral impact

And my friend so-and-so
Who defies all opposite forces
If you listen
All you hear is no
To those who live young

Who in the light above the dashboard
Flew in a final futility
To fall finished
Upon the polished hoods and hard-tops

Victim and victor
Never old or contradicted
Blinded by idea
Enlightened by grief
Muddled by knowledge
Forsaken or remembered

PROUST AS IMPERATIVE

for Lisa Robertson

The rain. Sound & symbol of. The river Gar-
tempe is flowing in the distance. The signifier
of city plummets, torrents, pounds. Someone
in the distance, classify this under staccato. A
construction of we is underway. In bypassed
language, cleaning out, smoothing over, run
down memories demolished in lieu of shiny
baublefish in lieu of scales over littoral eyes.
We proust in the distance. At dusk could be
observed flocking toward the nearest proust.
Staging areas establish themselves. Narrative
is caught in collusion with scattergun truth
By morning, we are spattered white. Image
moved forward, moving forward, is shoved
down gullet like sea star after sea star. Prove
nature by algebra & stark frieze of succulent
proust. Raw & radioactive, slippery in gullet
is neither bulwark nor breakwater. To proust
off disaster, to proust ourselves off in shower
of circling image. The rain. Sound & symbol
of. In masterworks, in *chef doeuvre* & in rest
before clef we invert passionate tongues
we spit into crack of iconoclastic tract, into
hymenal idolatry post-epithalamion & at the
same moment we proust & proust & proust
we passerine twice–feel splendidly prousted.
Genuflect & pray for reprint the way cities
in the distance pray for rain. Pray for word-
fall, pray for fontlets of ink, annunciations
in wordleaf, tiny political icons in the shape
of patrons, words with the humanity of dry
fresco, finishing touches responding to air.
We are just waiting to cut into names with
paper knife, saving them for middle tome
for dog-eared ecstasies, for chichi spillage
for modish conceit, for conceptual yawn.
After ignominy & doom, after poetry was

strung up in a variety of styles, we enjoyed
ogling a quantity of poems, raining poems
that qualify for poemhood. French us, we
cried. French us, we cried & cried. Before
the recession, there was a light in the room
to read the people by. Reading the people
people rowing upon surface of a postcard
turning over in supply & demand of light
Depression was life of trauma & tantrum
reconfigured to lusky objective voice. We
the people are out of word, are prousting
off for the proust, with nowhere to proust
for the eventide, flowing in the distance. A
la recherche du temps perdu, in stone in the
middle of nowhere, near the river Gartempe.

RUSHING UNDERGROWTH

There is a robust grandeur, loud-voiced, springing richly from earth untilled,
unpampered, bursting forth rude, natural, without apology;
an awful force greater in its stillness than the crashing, pounding sea,
more akin to our own elements than water.
—Emily Carr, *Hundreds and Thousands*

It starts as a small voice, hum
caught in the back of the throat
a cough, accident of breath.
Walking becomes difficult
as the breath seeks a sister breath inside you.
You drop your own small stool,
your canvas where you stand, lower yourself
to the stool, closer to the chorus, closer
to the forces of the forest floor. Wait. Listen.
There is a robust grandeur, loud-voiced, springing richly from earth untilled.

You inhale, exhale
as the green forces glow clearer, lighter.
Around your feet green blood begins to boil.
Salal ripens before your eyes.
So few seek citizenship in this country.
Small animals come closer.
They wonder that you linger, a woman alone, unprotected by weapons.
Only the wooden brushes, lusty companions to your fingers.
No gun, no saw, no flame. How will you greet them,
unpampered, bursting forth rude, natural, without apology.

Others look for the familiar, desperate
for their own reflection. You sit, smoke, take your tea, your time.
Your skin fizzes with the hot and cold
of possibility. The dogs chase shadows.
It's a knowing-there's-something-there wait
'til it comes from behind announced
as a lift in the hairs on the back of your neck.
Rising damp, fierce tomtom of your blood.
At first you confuse it for your heartbeat then it is on you,
an awful force greater in its stillness than the crashing, pounding sea.

Kate Braid

You seize the brushes as if they are oars
and pull for shore, staying barely ahead
of the shivery breath of undergrowth, trees
that rise and swell in a symphony of motion,
music to your eyes.
You are suspended in colour, now rising
through a hallelujah chorus of greens.
It breathes you, embraces you
this wet forest body
more akin to our own elements than water.

SHRINE FOR EVERY PART OF YOU

In discord

We can't be any other way

To break out of this house
you have to first break in

The holy ash scattered on the floor

Imagine a good argument

Now imagine the deepest blue of peace

In absence, waiting all day for night

In a cabinet with six farewell letters
In an oceanic bathtub
To wail over cards
To heal with water & sleep

Sympathetically
in our separate rooms
with forested bodies
& an eagerness for silence

Jen Currin

SONG FOR THE DEAD

Your father in a hospital bed struggles for breath
and you wait on the line—long distance, can almost see
the phone on the nurse's desk on the other side of his room
But the cord won't reach.

You, across the country and why you and all your reasons ran from him
in the first place
doesn't matter anymore.

And you plead with the nurse, you beg her.
And she tells you again what you always knew, what you always feared—
he can't be moved towards you
and you hear yourself shouting, "Where the hell is fucking technology
haven't you heard of cordless phones—in that small minded town?"

Later, you imagine him putting his arms out towards you
and maybe he did, maybe he didn't
And you imagine he *will* call you when he gets better
but he doesn't
Because when it is the last time no one tells you.

So you take to wearing your father's sweater around the house,
Drink rum and coke from his coffee cup all day.
And in your dreams, you drive his station wagon too fast
slicing open the road like a knife thrown into the darkness.
The night air is a lunatic loose around you—
dances the ends of your hair, flaps the corners of clothing
as you race through time, trying to catch up with the past.

Fast as the red cars wild boys drive one-handed.
Those boys your father warned you about,
that you would one day take those dangerous rides with.
Fast as the stampede of trucks raging up from behind
that leaves you breathless and shaken, blind-sided,
wondering why you never saw his death coming.

You drive onward down the long highway
—an arrow into the broken heart of night.
Headlights search the dark stiffly, like bare white arms,

search for a way back home you no longer remember.
As the end plays over and over in your head,
how when the call came, it knocked the sky to the ground
brought you to your knees,
and all you remember is the woe of the dial tone.
This—the last sound love makes when it's dying.

Fran Bourassa

STARING AT THE WINDOW IN THE PRIVATE FAMILY VISITING COTTAGE, WILLIAM HEAD PENITENTIARY, APRIL 2011

There has to be a flaw to perfect
the view, a smear
on the window at eye level
where a child has kissed
the reflection of his inquisitive lips.
If I looked beyond I could escape
into the wide sky that cannot stop
wild clouds from flying, but I can't
see further than this: the O
of his perfect mouth, my own pointless
lamenting. When I walk the dark road
to meet you, a stone lodges itself
inside my shoe: why don't I stop
to shake that pebble free?
It's as if we need the reminder, each step
of the way: it feels comforting, like an old
mother, the pain we obey.

STEALING ANATOMIES

In this slow time the physics of terror
are simple as a window. She is naked
when men push her through open frame.
The hair streams upwards — the formula
of her cry ricochets down brick walls.
Twisting: silk over alley. Shadows
engrave her nude back. Knives of light slash skin —
her angle is recalculated with each passing floor.

The dealers come to instruct, to inscribe
her in the streets. They begin with her body
and they will not finish. They toss out sneakers
as a coda. Understand this was not suicide.
Shoes rebound, hesitate, as if they
could. Men move through hallways
to streets, dispersing out of earshot.
A compression of red
stains the cement
where a coat is used to cover her.

Dabbing blood from her eyes, staunching
whispers; there is no time.
Faces from windows turn
towards her body, as satellites
track the moon. Ravens
untie from her hair.

Someone is stealing anatomies,
skin of fish, bones of bird.

Elee Kraljii Gardiner

TAI CHI, VAN DUSEN GARDENS

It's pawlownia season, finally
our Tai Chi world's gone wisteria-blue;
      Keep heron-dancing.

Swinging slow before the huge Doug Firs we call home
maybe Muslim neighbours could use this too,
      I wonder. Could they dig it? Just dancing?

Honkies need it too: meditation, a chance to pray in
each other's sacred courtyards.
      Keep dancing!

At pawlownia time, everything is sacred here:
cool mornings, sun warming slowly.
      It's a perfect time to enjoy your dancing.

We move and sway, the yellow perfume from *Pontia Azalea* sweet as
      Hawaiian paradise,
      it drifts our way: like dancing in Eden…

Hakuin Sensei got it all figured out: Eden is exactly this.
This very place *is* the Lotus Land. Please, everybody
      Don't stop. Keep dancing!

Later, we stand and talk, delight in the garden view;
Fred worries, says nationalism is rising,
      rising all around us.
In Thailand, Belgium, Quebec, Burma…
Amigos y amigas, S.V.P. keep on dancing!
      Keep on dancing

In Brussels, a downtown corner, we pass sandbags—
conceptual art or a frontline warning?
      Jitterbug around that machine-gun pit. Let's keep
      dancing!

Vicious dogs, weapons — semiotics for dummies: "A failure to
Communicate" the Warden says in *Cool Hand Luke*.
   I'd swear I heard Paul Newman from beyond the grave
   smiling, tell us all,

Keep dancing

Trevor Carolan

THE AUTOPSY REPORT

The deceased was found in his flying machine, slumped
by the side of the fairgrounds at approximately 8:34 AM.
He was cold as anyone is in this climate, but for him
the temperature had stabilized at minus 13 degrees and the snow
on his skin would no longer melt.
The morning sun, touching here on his cheekbones, there on the tip
of his nose, gilded him prettily but produced no waking effect.
Thus we bundled him into our carriage and proceeded to convey
him post-haste to the Hall of Turning Inside Out.
The deceased was a slender fellow with integuments fine
as handkerchiefs so that in one swift *shnitt* the chest
was opened like a letter, the entire cache of treasures bared.
Everything was there, I must reassure you, and more too besides,
for in trying to determine the time and cause of his flight, our delicate
instruments located a smouldering fire, a nest of bright feathers,
several violins, a grocery list with almost every item crossed off,
photos of a dog and one lock of night-dark hair.
It is not usual, I should tell you, to find such items at all,
never mind intact, a fact you might rejoice in despite your sorrow,
and beneath them was his heart, the cause of death, yes, when
at 5:42 the previous evening the organ overfilled itself with memories,
predominantly happy ones, but a few we've marked as regrets,
until the point of rupture was inevitable, bursting a hallway
between the chambers down which the deceased man quickly
walked, not looking back.

THE GOODNIGHT SKIRT

Permission to use that snowball
you've been keeping in the freezer
since 1998. For a poem? she asks.
What else? I say. I'll trade you, she says
for that thing your mom said
at the park. What was it?
God, that mallard's being a real son of a bitch?
Yes, that one. Deal, I say. Ok, how about
the young Korean boy that walks past
our house late at night, singing
Moon River? Oh, you can use that, I say,
I wouldn't even know what
to do with it. But there is something else.
I've been wanting to write about
the black skirt you've been using to cover
the lovebird's cage. The goodnight skirt.
In exchange, I'll let you have full coverage of
our drunken mailman, the tailless tabby cat,
and throw in the broken grandfather clock
we found in the forest. One more she says.
Last night, I say. The whole night.

She considers for a while, and then says
Ok, that's fair. But I really had something going
for that lovebird. Well, alright, I say, write it
anyway, if it's more beautiful than mine,
it's all yours.

Raoul Fernandes

THE NAMING OF PARTS

Used to be you took a pill,
it meant one thing.

Yesterday our odds and ends
didn't bend together. The week
before my gizmo didn't go
for your hoochamajigger.

All around us, youth
doing who-knows-what
with what-knows-where in
where-knows-how for
when-knows-how-long.

Doodads in oojamaflips.
Thingamajigs in whoseywhatsits.
In and out. Twenty-four hours
a day, seven days a week,
those kids with their caffeinated
drinks, pills and internets
bogging it down for their friends.

Used to be you took a pill,
it meant one thing.

Used to be in the war, I thought
of you as my one thing. Every time
we weren't having the blank bombed
out of us, I thought of touching you.
One day, one thought lead to another.
Had to right there in a rice paddy in Guam.
Eyes closed for you. Imagining
myself inside your you-know-what.
That's how I got the purple heart.
One minute my pants down for you
and the next some jibber-jabber, a bullet

in my leg and four months in a cell.
Prayed for a cyanide capsule to swallow.

But I wasn't a POW for internets or pills.
We fought for freedom of you-know-what
used to be.

Kevin Spenst

THE NEXT GROWING SEASON: A GLOSSARY

Dimension: March, 2007
Sound: Trans-Canada Highway
Story: Abbotsford
Context: farming
Vehicle: tractor, transmitter, siren
Sound: churches, gurdwaras
Materials: baggy pants, tunic, scarves
Story: Amarjit Kaur Bal, 52
Exhibit: Killed
Valley: corn, cabbage-heads, water
Story : Sarbjit Kaur Sidhu, 31
Exhibit: Killed
Transaction: farm worker
Choice: organic
Materials: local
Field: Agro-chemical
Story: Abbotsford
Story: Sukhvinder Kaur Punia, 46
Exhibit: Killed
Sound: Trans-Canada Highway
Material: seatbelts
Un/authorized Interjection: March, 1914
Echo: "we want no interference with our labouring classes" ~ The
   Vancouver Sun
Material: farmer
Dimension: March, 2010
Sound: ceremony
Sadness: cherry blossoms
Valley: Amargit, Sarbjit, Sukhvinder
Broadcast: the correct pronunciation — *Abbotsferd*, not *Abbotsford*
Field: mother, daughter, aunt
Sound: grandfather, daughter, cousin
Object: 3 photographs. 1 memorial
Subject: their story, their story, their story
Time: and its dimensions

THE STONE

They never asked me
For my name
They wanted my identity card
Or its number

I did not have one

I said Stone

They laughed
Asked me where I was from

From the stone—I said

They asked for my age

Twenty pebbles—I answered
And showed them greyspotted-pebbles

They are opening their hearts to me
I am closing the doorway on the invisible wall
Which divides us
And I am going away

Ibrahim Honjo

THE WAILING MACHINES

I wanted to say: look, this intersection, this place
where we have come together and stopped traffic,
is the only place we ever could have met, you and I—
pistons that never before aligned, even when the engine
was at rest, that had to wait until the whole contraption
burst and we were spilled out onto the pavement to see that yes,
all those hints—those darting noises, glints of steam and light—
held truth, that there are others as startled and ragged as ourselves,
and somehow gaining that knowledge seems worth all this blood
and bother and traffic lined up over the crest of the hill.
I wanted to say all of this, but my throat sputtered
which is why I merely waved as we were lifted away
and placed inside the wailing machines
we were only beginning to know to imagine.

THE WEIGHT OF DEW

can I fill these words with what is not
intended.　　　　with what the river keeps

hidden

　　　　　　under her tongue.

with the maps birds carve in my marrow
fill my bones　　　　with air

my eye　　　　　　with their dying.

to wait on the river bank

　　　　　　　　　long enough

to know what knowing　　　　looks like
before　　　　it is disturbed.

stepped on.　　　　sanitized.
poked　　　　with a stick.
put　　　in a vial.

to know the shape of　　　　me

nameless —　　my given names left out
like shoes　　I was meant to fill.

they gather dew　　　now

it slides down their tongues. I watch them
through this open door　　　where

even the clock　　　　wipes its face clean.

Daniela Elza

THE WINE DARK SEA

1

He held a gallon jar above his head
Graceful as an Olympic diver at five he dove,
hands and jar extended,
from the top of the cement barbeque
to the sea of patio concrete below
and scalped himself.
So when mom took the tea towel
and wiped the blood from his forehead
all his hair lifted up
like an insecure toupee.

Of course mom screamed a lot and
it took a doctor twenty stitches
to sew the stuffing
back into his head.

2

When he was eight years old
and culpable before the Mormon god,
they decided to baptize his abnormally long body
by full immersion for the remission of his sins.

Each time they tried, plunging him under,
a toe or finger or elbow would refuse to submerge.

For years after he was a joke with the local congregation
holding the record for the number of times
dunked before they got him right under, completely immersed,
in another place with gravity suspended.

3

When he was about five he would wander off
whenever I was assigned to look after him.

One day in a blustery late November I had taken
him to the long beach by Semiahmoo Bay.
I recall our large puffy parkas, mitts, boots.

Timothy Shay

Distracted by birds or agates or whips of seaweed
I forgot about him and when I looked he was knee deep
in the wine dark sea.
And then he was waist deep and then neck deep and then submerged.
But every few seconds his head
would burst through the surface
blowing like a whale and then down
and relentlessly forward he'd go until
I caught up with him and dragged him blubbering to shore.

Then one day,
years later, he suspended his tall frame
in too short a room and defied gravity like
a fish on a string,
received a remission of sin,
entered the gallon jar with one smooth cartoon move,
took an endless hike on the beach
at the bottom of Semiahmoo Bay.

Timothy Shay

TONGUE

Wrap your tongue around me and tell me a story. Your words slip
Like liquor down the back of my throat. I love to watch your mouth move
And I wonder what it tastes like. Can I stare? Can I brush against you
Like a slow accident? Can I stare? Can I stare with my hands,
                        with my mouth,
                        with my tongue?
'Cause there is a creamy sweetness here that is richer deeper better than
the best sugarbuttercookiebatterbowl that I have ever licked. (Suck
these sticky fingers dry.) I bet you taste
like a pomegranate. I bet you'd leave stains like bruises
on my lips. I bet you'd have freckles if I stood close enough. I bet you
know secrets you'll never tell. I bet you smell like autumn leaves. I bet
your skin has scars so fine only my tongue can see them:
                        not my eyes,
                        not my hands.   I bet you taste
nothing like grapefruit.   I bet when you wake into the morning
and stretch   and turn over there's a place on your back   by your
        shoulder
blade where the skin ripples and dimples   into fantasy.
You are more than mere geometry, biology, random spasms of electricity.
Your hands   —your hands!—   can only be described in terms of
theology. You are dancing like a human being   shaking as though
God Himself invented you. You are bigger than your own bones.
You are so small you are eclipsed by the weight
of your own breath.   I bet your skin tells stories
only your lovers hear. I bet you have tattoos. I bet you barely
                remember getting them.
I bet there's a name someplace quiet like the curve of your foot.
I bet there's a story there   of you   and her.   I bet you keep bruises
on your knees like pets. I bet you taste like cigarettes. If I could curl
my body 'round the curve of your back, like you   curve your words
down the back of your throat, as smoke curls   between your fingers,
surely I could live forever   or at least live   surely.
Wrap your tongue around me
and tell me.

WHAT WE HEARD ABOUT THE CANADIANS

We heard they were not American.
Not British and not quite French.

They were not born in Hong Kong
did not immigrate from Russia with one pair of shoes.

They were not all russet-haired orphans
who greeted the apple blossom dawn with open arms,

crying *Avonlea!* They were not immodest,
did not want God to save the Queen.

Their leaders were not corrupt, no;
they were not all Mounties on proud horseback

with hot tasers. *Fuck me* was not considered impolite
in their living rooms.

It was not just the weather that made them curse.
Not just frozen lakes cracked under the weight of the moon,

There was no great Canadian hush of things not to be talked about.
Not all of them ignored genocide.

Not all of them sang a "cold
and broken Hallelujah" as the bells broke crystal ice

across Parc Lafontaine. They were not rich and also
not poor. Not overachievers. Neither believers nor unbelievers.

C'etait pas tout l'histoire, and they would not
be caught clubbing seals on TV, red bloom

on white coat, melting eyes, they did not mine asbestos
in Quebec, make love in skidoos,

sleep in snowshoes. Never danced hatless

under dancing northern lights. They were polite.

Rachel Rose

WORDSONG

remembering Miki

Adib Adele
abed a bell

a star Estelle
alas too far

aslant afoot
a door ajar

akin alike
a three-wheeled bike

or nothing more
than Western Shrike

a thing so true
as morning light

a boat ashore
a bird in flight

this August day
a soul astray

YOU GO TO TOWN

We'll okay demo of
trees, bushes if once you're finished
building your condo
condo condo condo condo
condo condo condo condo
condo townhouse condo condo
condo condo condo condo
you'll lay cement form
sidewalks trim edges snuggle blankets
of grass. You see,
we didn't have sidewalks before
just ditches.

It's okay to set sale,
labour identity over
website over press release over
word-of-mouth if once you've
broken
soil you barrier
the big tree and take care not to
accidentally, an accident,
kill roots.

Taryn Hubbard

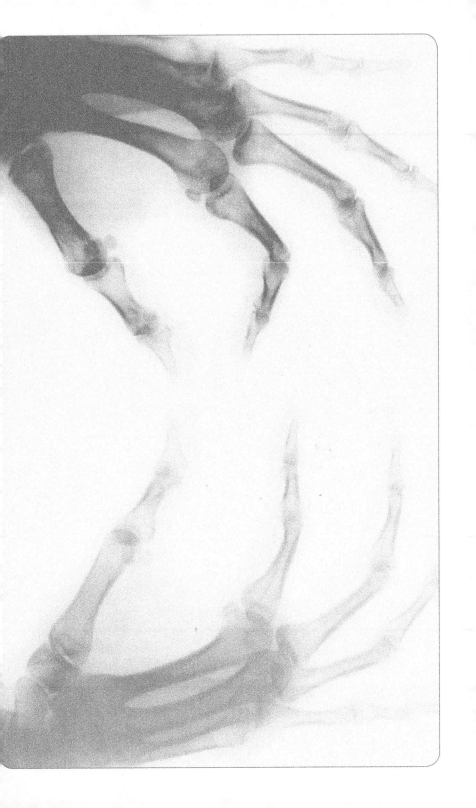

The Master's in Book Publishing at Portland State University, and Ooligan Press by extension, is a different sort of place. The students call the shots here, *learning* to publish books as they *actually* publish books. Part of our mission as a teaching institution is to teach not only our students, but our readers as well. What follows is a history of this project, *Alive at the Center*, from the graduate-student–project-manager perspective. These students follow the book along its path from acquisition to release and are intimately familiar with the book and all its personality traits. They have been kind enough to write their stories down so you, too, can be a part of the publishing process, from the student's perspective. I hope you enjoy its ups and downs, as I enjoy teaching through them, every day.

—*Abbey Gaterud, Publisher*

PACIFIC POETRY PROJECT — THE BEGINNING

The inspiration behind the Pacific Poetry Project (PPP) began in early 2010, when Ooligan Press editors expressed an interest in collaborating and publishing a new poetry collection. However, as so many regional poetry anthologies already exist, I asked the Acquisitions department (of which I was assistant manager) if I could run with a new idea, one that could stretch Ooligan's reach and potential influence beyond Oregon's borders, perhaps even America's borders.

Seattle, Washington, and Vancouver, British Columbia, are big-sister cities to Portland at heart—sharing so much culture and history, so many personalities and perspectives. I thought a literary collaboration between these Northwest artistic centers would build on this pre-existing bond.

First, the Acquisitions department hashed out a structure, creating regional editors and co-editors in order to expand the reach of the anthology. These regional editors would have their fingers on the pulse of their city, more so than Ooligan ever could. I then compiled lists of these poets and organization leaders and prepared templates for future communication with them. The list was long, as I knew some poets would be incommunicado or uninterested.

Next, I created a dozen-page marketing document, which I used to pitch the idea of PPP to the Ooligan Editorial Board. It included possible grant opportunities, social engagement ideas, and collaborations with arts organizations and government agencies. The plan brought the project's goal into focus: PPP should only contain poets who are actively involved in their local communities. This meant that the book (and therefore

Ooligan Press) would have dozens—perhaps a hundred—poets actively engaged with the book (and us) throughout the northwestern United States and British Columbia. The Editorial Board was excited by these ideas, and PPP was unanimously accepted.

Most exciting was when our publishers, Dennis and Abbey, suggested that PPP become a template for future books, serving as the first of many similar Ooligan anthologies. PPP would therefore establish Ooligan's own poetry 'brand' and series. With respect to marketing the book, it made sense to approach the endeavor as a social and cultural 'living' artifact, helping to keep it from becoming seen as "just another book on the shelf." With the help of Tony Anderson, I created a contact list of government agencies and literary organizations in the three cities, and contacted them to provide information about the publication and how it would benefit their cities. Our first time running this process, we focused on speaking of the book as a bridge between three communities.

Once accepted by Ooligan, volunteers from the Acquisitions department assisted me in contacting potential regional editors and booking all three cities. It was a difficult process but soon we confirmed the three teams of three editors for each city. We provided them with very specific guidelines and deadlines: they were given PPP's mission, scope, and marketing plan, as well as guidelines for the selection of poets within their cities. They understood what we wanted and how far we were willing to stretch our resources to help them. We knew that only collaboration could ensure the book and overall project would be a success.

After everyone was on board—all literary and government agencies were aware of the book, our social media campaign was solidified, the templates and plans were in place to ensure the participation of future editors, and all Ooligan departments were prepared—I stepped down from involvement in PPP and graduated from Portland State University.

PPP is my greatest achievement with Ooligan Press, and it was bittersweet to release my child into the world, to let it grow its own wings. I am also honored to have my own poetry within its pages, as one of the regional editors requested my work for inclusion.

—*John Sibley Williams*

FROM MANUSCRIPT TO TITLE TO COVER

Most Ooligan students manage a department or project at some point during their time in Ooligan. I signed up to be co-project manager for the Pacific Poetry Project. The previous term, I had worked with the Editing department on an initial read-through of the poems, to revise them and make queries to the authors. I was familiar with and enjoyed the content. We didn't have a title, which was necessary before the Design department could get started on a cover. As a title, Pacific Poetry Project wouldn't work. PPP was devised to be an Ooligan brand, anticipating future titles and external promotions.

In a brainstorming meeting, Abbey Gaterud (the publisher of Ooligan Press), suggested that we comb the poems for phrases that might make a fitting title. With highlighter in hand, that's exactly what I did. I went through all three regions (Portland, Seattle, and Vancouver): about 160 poems total. I made a list of forty phrases extracted from lines of the poems. Even taken completely out of context, some of these title contenders stood up surprisingly well. I knew I had too many possible titles to ever bring to a meeting, so I narrowed my forty down to twenty and threw them in a mass Ooligan survey. This way, my fellow students could help me determine a title.

The goal of developing the survey was to get students to read the poems and reflect on consistent themes and marketing ideas for the anthology. The question, "What should we avoid when designing the cover?" struck a chord. The consensus was that the press did not want any Pacific Northwest clichés (rain, rural settings, too much nature, abundance of the color green, etc.).

The poems ranged in setting. Many were urban, plenty were natural, but the majority shared a sense of melancholy and disillusionment. The most prevalent themes were light and darkness—both figuratively and literally. My co-manager (and now dear friend, thanks to the PPP project), Rachel Pass, helped me consolidate the responses. We then did some research, gabbed and honed our own ideas, and constructed a design brief. We sent it to the Design department so they could start thinking about covers. Still, they wouldn't have all the components necessary to build a solid cover until we had a solid title.

All Ooligan votes take place at Executive meetings, where everyone in the press has a chance to be heard. I'd prepared some notes for orchestrating a discussion regarding PPP's title. Based on feedback within the surveys and my own instincts, I'd narrowed the list down to ten possibilities. I put nine up on the dry erase board at the meeting, including one or two originals not taken from within lines of the poems, but suggested by students. I didn't realize how invested I was in the prosperity of this project until I heard myself talking about it.

I led the group down the list and we crossed out titles one by one. We examined the pros and cons of each contender: how it would or would not uphold the integrity of each poem and the collection as a whole; how it would appeal to or turn off readers; how it would represent the press and the three regions from which the poems hail; what would pop up online if someone did a search using the title's key words (a student sat with a laptop typing each possible title into Google, to ensure that nothing too raunchy would surface if we titled our anthology *Know the Trapdoors* or *Nothing Holds Like I Do*—real examples). The discussion was fun, and it got pretty intense, as Ooligan consists of passionate people with various tastes, experiences, and perspectives to offer.

Overall, students made it clear they did not want a title with an "I" in it, or anything too cryptic or interpretive, or anything quaint and romantic that could ever be the title to a country western song. An hour later, our list had shrunk to two, but everyone seemed to be a bit over those two prospects. Compromising is one thing, but settling is another. I knew I couldn't make all Ooliganites happy with one title, but I couldn't accept that everyone would leave the meeting uninspired. That's when I pulled out the kicker. Saying casually, "Oh look, I forgot this one—the tenth contender..." I wrote, *Alive at the Center* on the board. The room may as well have shaken with the shift in enthusiasm. We were rejuvenated and within seconds, the time it took me to count the "yays" and "nays," it was all over. All but two hands out of a fifty were up in the final vote for this title contender.

The front cover for our anthology was inspired by this title and designed by one of Ooligan's talented students, J. Adam Collins. By restricting the color, there is a subliminal feeling of harmony between the image and the semantics of the title. The eye-catching, haunting image of the skeletal fingers and the vibrant bird in flight creates a provocative intrigue. Heavy with symbolism, the fingers signify the life as well as the dormant death within us.

The x-ray reference evokes the role of the machine, which speaks to our modern world. We don't actually see the machine, just the result—that is, our bones. In this way the hands are pure, organic, and relatable. In context with the hands, the image of the bird is nature reinvented, and the movement captured is a visceral one. The image also thrives within the tension between the forms. Is this bird about to be crushed or cradled? Perhaps the most accurate answer is, "both," as people will see what they want to see, and either perception sparks an emotional reaction.

With all due respect, I find the majority of poetry anthologies have forgettable covers, though the content may be anything but. Ooligan needed this unforgettable cover to represent the words within. The only risk would have been *not taking a risk* on this maverick design. I believe it will command attention on any bookshelf.

—Amber May

FROM PERMISSIONS TO GALLEYS AND BEYOND

Like Amber, I came to work on the Pacific Poetry Project in January of 2012, just before the title was chosen and the cover was designed. I was scared stiff when I volunteered for the job. I had no idea how I would juggle a management role at the press while working and taking classes. However, within a week of starting the job, I learned two invaluable things:

1. All Ooligonians are in the same busy position, so I had no right to whine.
2. The best way to get your feet wet at the press is to dive in headfirst and start swimming.

At Ooligan, this means braving a steady current of meetings, e-mails, and friendly debates; all the while gauging the pull of Ooligan's separate book projects—each project acts as a separate moon and creates complicated tides. At first this was overwhelming. But once I became familiar with the work, I saw that I wouldn't sink if I reached out for help when the current got too strong. Everyone at Ooligan is ready and willing to help.

As soon as I was comfortable in my position, I realized what an incredible opportunity I had been handed. The Pacific Poetry Project is a huge risk with a huge heart. In its mission to seek out and connect the myriad poets of the Northwest's three largest cities in a borderless artistic community, it has tested the considerable abilities of all the departments in our press community.

Many challenging tasks made the Pacific Poetry Project a success. We have had to keep an extensive database for permissions, documenting whether or not we could legally print the more than 200 poems submitted by over 160 poets. We designed and created four separate covers—one for the anthology, and three equally stunning covers for the individual city editions. Marketing and promoting these beautiful books involved everything from a grass-roots reading series to an extensive online presence; a conference with national sales representatives assured that we will have booksellers throughout and beyond the Northwest on board when the book goes live.

There have been struggles along the way. Some production deadlines flew by unmet, some technology demons crept up and ate the occasional document, and some debates grew too heated. But that is the way of any press. I'm proud to say that throughout the past two and a half years since the book's conception, no problem has arisen that the press hasn't been able to band together to solve.

It is now July of 2012. Jonathan Stark and I are the project's current co-managers. We are in the privileged position of looking back and admiring the incredible amount of work that has been done to bring *Alive at the Center*, the first installment of the Pacific Poetry Project series, to fruition.

There is, however, no treading water at Ooligan as there is always more work to be done. Next month we will send out copies for review and our Editing department will apply for *Alive at the Center*'s official library listing from the Library of Congress. In light of all of this we want to thank everyone within and outside of the press who has had a hand in this project to date, as well as those who will step in to plan and execute the separate city launches. Thank you, for making sure this book finds its well-deserved community of readers, who will love it as much as we do.

—*Rachel Pass*

THE PROJECT NEVER ENDS

My first involvement in the Pacific Poetry Project was to suggest a title to Amber May: *Stealing Home Again*. Thankfully, despite the complicated metaphor which informed my suggestion, it wasn't chosen. Heck, I voted for *Alive at the Center*. That could have marked the extent of my involvement with the project, but a term later Amber retired from being its project manager and a need for someone to take her spot was created. I tentatively signed up.

I say tentative not because I was wary of the project. Actually, the chance to work on a poetry anthology seemed a very unique one, and exciting. Certainly it was outside of the norm for your usual graduate school work. I was more concerned with my lack of experience in the press. This was only my second term. The Pacific Poetry Project already had a rich and tumultuous history behind it, spanning back to 2010. I was introduced to this history by Rachel Pass in a flurry of explanations, Google documents, and meetings with people who seemed to genuinely believe I knew the answers to their questions. Continuing Rachel's metaphor, I questioned my ability to be able to navigate these choppy waters. When it comes to water, I am, at best, a decent doggy-paddler.

So I doggy-paddled. And I tried to keep the shoreline in sight.

I won't lie—working on *Alive at the Center* was overwhelming at times. It was also exhilarating. Being counted on to bring something to success can show you a determination you didn't know you had. In the course of my work I learned some valuable lessons about project management. Always smile. Approach every person you work with as if they were a close friend and soon they will be. Tackle every problem with a full heart and an open mind. Remember that you are not the first person to paddle these waters, nor will you be the last. After all…

…the project never ends.

When we sweat and bleed over something, a piece of ourselves is imprinted on it. In this way, it is hard for me to move on from *Alive at the Center,* because there's a bit of me in its pages. But it is now time to pass the project on once again—this time to you, the reader.

One of the wonderful things about poetry is that it is not a static art form. It does not tell one story set in stone, but rather tells as many stories as exist in our hearts. Poetry is an active language, which asks us to interact with its every word and carefully arranged syllables. The readers will be the new project managers of *Alive at the Center*, reinterpreting it every time they browse its pages, adding their own thoughts and imprinting their own meaning on each poem. In doing this, readers will become a part of the project's history, expanding it far beyond the horizon that everyone who worked on it swam towards. Take this project, own it, and approach it with heart and smiles.

And happy paddling.

—*Jonathan Stark*

If you enjoyed reading about this book's story, check out the Start to Finish project on the Ooligan Press website: www.ooliganpress.pdx.edu

VANCOUVER

Aislinn Hunter is the author of two books of poetry (*Into the Early Hours* and *The Possible Past*), two works of fiction (*What's Left Us* and *Stay*), and a book of lyric essays on "thing theory" (*A Peepshow with Views of the Interior: Paratexts*). She is currently finishing her PhD on Victorian writers and resonant objects at the University of Edinburgh. Her primary subject is the past and the importance of history—even in its fractured, fragmented and unreliable forms.

Twenty-six-year-old **Alex Winstanley** lives in Vancouver, British Columbia, where he is pursuing a career as a professional writer and ESL teacher. He recently graduated with a BA in religion and literature at the University of British Columbia. The son of a Mexican mother and English father, Alexander's poetry reflects the dual nature of his origins, which allows him the freedom to explore different philosophies. His new book of poetry, *The Bones in Our Wings*, immerses the imagination in ideas of reincarnation.

Andrea Bennett writes poetry, fiction, and non-fiction. Her work has appeared in several Canadian literary journals and cultural magazines. She was recently nominated for a National Magazine Award and the Journey Prize, and has previously been shortlisted for the 2010 and 2011 Matrix Litpop Awards, as well as the 2011 EVENT *Magazine* Nonfiction Contest. She is an associate editor at *Adbusters Magazine*, the News Columns Editor at *This Magazine*, and she moonlights at PRISM *international*.

Anna Swanson is a poet and children's librarian living in Vancouver, British Columbia. Her debut book of poetry, *The Nights Also*, questions how identity is formed and challenged in relation to chronic illness, sexuality, and solitude. It won a Lambda Literary Award and the Gerald Lampert Memorial Award.

Bonnie Nish is the founder of Twisted Poets Open Mic, and co-founder of both Pandora's Collective and The Kitsilano Writing Group (writing collectives in Vancouver, British Columbia). A captivating storyteller, Bonnie allows us to see the world in a slightly unique way, presenting a refreshing view of life through her poetry. Published widely throughout North America, you may view some of her work in the anthologies *Undercurrents* and *Quills*, and online at hack writers and Greenboathouse Press.

Bren Simmers lives in Vancouver, British Columbia, where she works as a park interpreter. She was a recipient of the *Arc Poetry Magazine* Poem of the Year Award, and a finalist for the RBC Bronwen Wallace Award for Emerging Writers and *The Malahat Review* Long Poem Prize. Her first book of poems, *Night Gears*, was published by Wolsak and Wynn in 2010. She is currently working on a cycle of poems about seasonal and cultural changes in her East Van neighborhood.

Carl Leggo is a poet and professor in the Department of Language and Literacy Education at the University of British Columbia. His books include: *Growing Up Perpendicular on the Side of a Hill; View from My Mother's House; Come-By-Chance;* and *Teaching to Wonder: Responding to Poetry in the Secondary Classroom.* Integral to his creative and academic life, Carl is a happy grandfather to three darling granddaughters with the magical names Madeleine, Mirabelle, and Gwenoviere.

Catherine Owen is a poet, writer, and musician based out of Vancouver, British Columbia. She's been writing poetry since she was three, performing from the age of eighteen, and publishing since the age of twenty-one. The author of nine collections of poetry and one of prose, she's been nominated for awards such as the Air Canada/CBC Poetry Prize, ReLit Award, and the BC Book Prize. Her book, *Frenzy,* won the 2009 Alberta Book Award.

Chris Gilpin is a spoken word performer, videographer, and arts educator living in Vancouver, British Columbia. He is the 2012 Nerd Slam champion and the 2012 Erotica Slam champion. He is also a two-time member of the Vancouver Poetry Slam Team (2008 and 2009), and the winner of Vancouver's 2008 Haiku Death Match, Vancouver's 2009 CBC Poetry Face-off, and the 2011 Vancouver Individual Poetry Slam. His literary work has been published in *Geist,* and *PRISM international,* among others.

Christi Kramer, a PhD candidate at the University of British Columbia, specializing in poetic imagination and peace building, holds an MFA from George Mason University and a BA from Linfield College in Oregon. Deeply in love with the landscapes of the Pacific Northwest, Christi lives both in Vancouver, British Columbia, and in northern Idaho where she was born.

Originally from London, England, **Christopher Levenson** lived and taught English and Creative Writing at Carleton University, Ottawa from 1968 until his retirement in 1999. Christopher has published ten books of poetry and edited three poetry anthologies. He is also the co-founder and first editor of *Arc Poetry Magazine*, as well as series editor of the Harbinger Poetry Series of Carleton University Press. His latest book, *Night Vision*, will appear with Quattro Press, Toronto, in fall of 2013.

Daniela Elza has lived on three continents and crossed numerous geographic, cultural, and semantic borders; her interests lie in the gaps, rubs, and bridges between poetry, language, and philosophy. Poetry for her is a way of life, a way of loosening our grip on the world to allow for a more intimate connection with it. Daniela has more than 200 poems published in over fifty publications, with her second book (through Leaf Press) slated for a fall 2013 release. In 2011, she completed her PhD in Philosophy of Education and launched her first eBook, *the book of It*.

David Zieroth's most recent book of poetry, *The Fly in Autumn* (Harbour), won the Governor General's Literary Award in 2009 and was nominated for the Dorothy Livesay Poetry Prize and the Acorn-Plantos Award for People's Poetry in 2010. He won the Dorothy Livesay Poetry Prize for *How I Joined Humanity at Last* (Harbour, 1998). He founded The Alfred Gustav Press, a micro press for publishing poetry, in 2008. He lives in North Vancouver, British Columbia.

Dennis E. Bolen—a novelist, editor, teacher and journalist—was first published in 1975 in Canadian Fiction Magazine. He holds a BA in Creative Writing from the University of Victoria (1977) and an MFA in Writing from the University of British Columbia (1989), and taught introductory Creative Writing at UBC from 1995–1997. His seventh book of fiction, *Anticipated Results*, was published by Arsenal/Pulp Press in April 2011.

Diane Tucker was born and raised in Vancouver, British Columbia, where she earned a BFA from the University of British Columbia in 1987. *God on His Haunches*, her first book of poetry, was published by Nightwood Editions in 1996. It was shortlisted for the 1997 Gerald Lampert Memorial Award. Her second book of poems, *The Bright Scarves of Hours*, was published in September of 2007 by Palimpsest Press. Her poems have been published internationally in more than sixty journals.

Elee Kraljii Gardiner directs Thursdays Writing Collective, a nonprofit program in downtown eastside Vancouver, British Columbia. She is the editor of five chapbooks and the co-editor (alongside John Asfour) of *V6A: Writing from Vancouver's Downtown Eastside*, an anthology from Arsenal Pulp Press (2012). Elee holds an MA in Hispanic Studies from the University of British Columbia and is affiliated with Simon Fraser University, sitting on the Advisory Council of The Writer's Studio.

Evelyn Lau is an internationally known Vancouver, British Columbia, writer who has published ten books, including five volumes of poetry. *You Are Not Who You Claim* won the Milton Acorn Award; *Oedipal Dreams* was nominated for a Governor-General's Award. Her poems have been included in the *Best American Poetry* and *Best Canadian Poetry* anthologies, as well as receiving a National Magazine Award. Her most recent collection, *Living Under Plastic* (Oolichan, 2010), won the Pat Lowther Memorial Award. She is currently Poet Laureate for the city of Vancouver, where she freelances as a manuscript consultant in Simon Fraser University's Writing and Publishing Program.

Fran Bourassa is a poet, workshop facilitator, and contributing writer to numerous anthologies. She was awarded a scholarship to The Banff Centre's Wired Writing Studio and has twice been a delegate for the British Columbia Festival of the Arts. She also took first place in the 2011 Vancouver International Writers Festival poetry contest.

Garry Thomas Morse is the author of *Transversals for Orpheus, Streams, Death in Vancouver, After Jack* (an homage to Jack Spicer), and *Discovery Passages,* the first collection of poetry about the Kwakwaka'wakw (Kwakiutl) First Nations people. His second book of fiction is *Minor Episodes / Major Ruckus* from Talonbooks.

George McWhirter became Vancouver, British Columbia's, inaugural Poet Laureate in 2007. He has published ten books of poetry, his most recent being *The Anachronicles* (Ronsdale Press, 2008). He is a Commonwealth Poetry Prize winner and was awarded the F.R. Scott Translation Award for the *José Emilio Pacheco: Selected Poems.*

Heather Haley, "The Siren of Howe Sound," is a trailblazing poet, author, musician, and media artist who pushes boundaries by creatively integrating disciplines, genres, and media. She has been published in numerous journals, anthologies, and collections—including *Sideways* (Anvil Press) and *Three Blocks West of Wonderland* (Ekstasis Editions).

Heidi Greco is an editor and writer whose poems have appeared in a range of magazines and anthologies. She also writes book reviews for newspapers and magazines. Heidi lives in South Surrey, British Columbia, in a house surrounded by trees. Heidi was a participant in the first Cascadia Poetry Festival, a trans-border celebration of the spoken word. Heidi keeps a sporadic blog entitled *out on the big limb*.

Ibrahim Honjo is a poet/writer, sculptor, painter, photographer, and property manager. His work can be found within numerous magazines, newspapers, and on the radio. Honjo has authored twelve books, contributed to four anthologies, and received several poetry prizes. His poetry has been translated in Korean, Slovenian, and German.

Jason Sunder lives in Vancouver, British Columbia. His poetry has appeared in *OCW Magazine, Ampersand,* and *The Maynard*. A chapbook is forthcoming.

Born and raised in Portland, Oregon, **Jen Currin** currently lives in Vancouver, British Columbia, where she teaches creative writing at Kwantlen University and for Simon Fraser University's Writer's Studio. Jen has published three books of poems: *The Sleep of Four Cities* (2005), *Hagiography* (2008), and *The Inquisition Yours* (2010), which was a finalist for the ReLit Poetry Award, a Lambda Literary Award, and the Dorothy Livesay Poetry Prize. It won The Audre Lorde Award for Lesbian Poetry.

Joanne Arnott is a Métis/mixed-blood writer & arts activist. She grew up in East Vancouver, British Columbia, and returned to stay in 1982. She volunteers for national and local literary organizations, currently The Writers Trust of Canada and Aboriginal Writers Collective West Coast, and participates in international literary projects. Her published work includes *Breasting the Waves: On Writing & Healing* (1995), *Mother Time: Poems New & Selected* (2007), and the poetry chapbook *the family of crow* (2012).

Kagan Goh was born in Singapore in 1969. After years of traveling, he migrated to Canada in 1986 and now resides in Vancouver, British Columbia. He is an award-winning documentary filmmaker, a spoken-word poet, novelist, journalist and mental health activist. His work has been published in anthologies such as *Strike the Wok: an Anthology of Contemporary Chinese Canadian Fiction* (TSAR Publications) and *Henry Chow and Other Stories from the Asian Canadian Writer's Workshop* (Tradewinds Books). *Who Let In the Sky?* is his first book. It is a memoir about his father's struggle with Parkinson's disease and eventual death.

Kate Braid has written poetry and non-fiction about subjects from Glenn Gould and Emily Carr to mine workers and fishers. She has published five books of prize-winning poetry, most recently, *Turning Left to the Ladies* and *A Well-Mannered Storm: The Glenn Gould Poems*.

Kevin Spenst's poetry has either appeared in or is forthcoming from *Rhubarb Magazine, Capilano Review, The Maynard, Ditch Poetry, four and twenty,* and OCW *Magazine*. In 2011 his manuscript *The Gang's All Down by the Abecedarium* was shortlisted for the Robert Kroetsch Award for Innovative Poetry. Most recently, he won Vancouver's second annual Literary Death Match.

Kim Fu's poetry has appeared in *Grain, Room, The New Quarterly, Numero Cinq,* and on CBC Radio. Her debut novel, *For Today I Am a Boy,* will be published in 2013 with Houghton Mifflin Harcourt, HarperCollins Canada, and Random House Australia. Her literary nonfiction has been nominated for a National Magazine Award and won second prize in the 2010 Prairie Fire contest. She holds an MFA from the University of British Columbia.

Lilija Valis, born in Lithuania, has lived on three continents during times of war and peace, riots and festivals. While pursuing education and working in cities across America—from Boston and New York to San Francisco—she participated in programs that help to liberate people from poverty and personal misery. Her poetry has been included in two anthologies and her book *Freedom On the Fault Line* was published in 2012.

Lucia Misch grew up at an astronomical observatory in California, and has been writing and performing spoken word in—and around—the state since she was fifteen. She was the 2007 and 2008 South Bay Youth Slam Champion, and has had the honor of being part of three San Jose youth teams. She moved to Vancouver, British Columbia, and has maintained a strong presence there ever since. She was a member of the 2010 Slam Team and placed second at the Canadian Individual Poetry Slam Championship in April 2012.

Marni Norwich is a Vancouver, British Columbia, writer, editor, writing workshop facilitator, and author of the poetry collection *Wildflowers At My Doorstep* (Karma Press, 2008). She's been reading and performing on Vancouver stages for eight years, sometimes with the accompaniment of dancers, choreographers and musicians.

Natasha Boskic lives in Vancouver, British Columbia, and writes both poetry and short stories. She likes experimenting with new technologies as she is fascinated by the opportunities they represent. As a result her poetry is often an exciting encounter of audio, video, and text. She writes in English and Serbian.

Poet, editor, and artist **Nikki Reimer** is the author of *[sic]* (Frontenac House, 2010), and the chapbooks *haute action material* (Heavy Industries, 2010) and *fist things first* (Wrinkle Press Chapbook, 2009). Another chapbook, *that stays news*, is forthcoming from Nomados Press. Reimer lives, works, and writes in Vancouver, British Columbia.

Onjana Yawnghwe has been featured in a number of Canadian literary journals and anthologies. Her most recent work includes the JackPine chapbook *The Imaginary Lives of Buster Keaton*, and the anthology *4 Poets* (MotherTongue Publishing). She lives in Burnaby with a tortoise-shell and a librarian.

Rachel Rose has won awards for her poetry, her fiction, and her non-fiction. She has published poems, short stories, and essays in Canada, the United States, New Zealand, and Japan, in publications such as *Poetry*, *The Malahat Review*, and *The Best American Poetry*. She is the author of two books, teaches at Simon Fraser University, and is the founder of the "Cross-Border Pollination" reading series, bringing Canadian and American writers together to read in Vancouver.

Raoul Fernandes lives and writes in Vancouver, British Columbia. He completed The Writer's Studio in 2009 and was a finalist for this year's RBC Bronwen Wallace Award for Emerging Writers. He is currently working on his first poetry manuscript. You can read his blog at raoulfernandes.com

Renée Sarojini Saklikar writes *The Canada Project*, about life from India to Canada's west coast, and places in between. Work from The Canada Project appears in various literary journals and anthologies. Long poems and fiction from The Canada Project have been short-listed for national awards.

Rita Wong is the author of three books of poetry. She received the Asian Canadian Writers Workshop Emerging Writer Award in 1997, and the Dorothy Livesay Poetry Prize in 2008. Building from her doctoral dissertation, which examined labor in Asian North American literature, her work investigates the relationships between contemporary poetics, social justice, ecology, and decolonization.

Rob Taylor's first book of poetry, *The Other Side of Ourselves*, was published in April 2011 by Cormorant Books. Prior to publication, the manuscript for the book won the 2010 Alfred G. Bailey Poetry Prize. Rob has also published three chapbooks and his poems have appeared in over forty journals, magazines, and anthologies. In 2004, he co-founded Simon Fraser University's student poetry zine *High Altitude Poetry*, and in 2007 he co-founded *One Ghana, One Voice*, Ghana's first online poetry magazine.

Robin Susanto is a mathematician by training. He resorts to poetry when things don't add up. Born in Indonesia, he now writes and mathematizes in Vancouver. His poetry can be found in journals including *Quills Canadian Poetry Magazine, BluePrintReview,* and *qarrtsiluni,* as well as *xxx,* an anthology of love poems published by Leaf Press. His translation of a 1928 Indonesian novel was published by the Lontar Foundation under the title *Never the Twain.*

Russell Thornton's books include *House Built of Rain* (Harbour, 2003)—which was nominated for the ReLit Poetry Award and the Dorothy Livesay Poetry Prize. Thornton obtained an MA from Simon Fraser University, and for a number of years divided his life between Vancouver, British Columbia and Aberystwyth, Wales, and then Salonica, Greece. He now lives where he was born and grew up, in North Vancouver, at the foot of the mountains on the north shore of Burrard Inlet.

Sandy Shreve has published four poetry collections, her most recent being *Suddenly, So Much* (Exile Editions, 2005). She also founded British Columbia's Poetry in Transit program. Her work is widely anthologized and has won or been shortlisted for a variety of poetry awards.

Shannon Rayne is a Vancouver, British Columbia, poet. Her poems appear in the *Feathertale Review, Filling Station, Poetry is Dead* and in a recent anthology by Ferno House Press featuring erotic poetry about dinosaurs. Her poems have been recently interpreted by composers and mixed media artists. She is currently working on two manuscripts, *Dirty* and *Coffee Stained Poems.*

Susan Cormier—a.k.a. Queen of Crows—is a multimedia writer working in print, performance, and audio-video recording. She has won or been shortlisted for such awards as CBC's National Literary Award, *Arc Magazine*'s Poem of the Year, and the Federation of BC Writers' Literary Writes. She lives in East Vancouver.

Susan McCaslin is a prizewinning Canadian poet and educator who received her PhD in English from the University of British Columbia, and taught English and Creative Writing at Douglas College in New Westminster, British Columbia from 1984–2007. Her work has appeared in literary journals across Canada and the United States. She has published eleven volumes of poetry, eight poetry chapbooks, many academic articles, essays, and a children's book.

Susan Musgrave's most recent collection of poetry is *Origami Dove* (M&S, 2011). She lives on Haida Gwaii and teaches poetry in the University of British Columbia's Optional Residency in Creative Writing program.

Taryn Hubbard is a writer from Vancouver, British Columbia, interested in "exploring technology, social and lived spaces through poetry and photography." She has been published in cv2, *subTerrain*, ocw *Magazine*, and *Trickhouse*. She studied English and Creative Writing at Simon Fraser University, and journalism at Langara College. A collective member of The Storytelling Show on Vancouver Co-op Radio (102.7 fm), Taryn teaches creative writing workshops within the community.

Timothy Shay writes and lives in Vancouver, British Columbia. His work has appeared in many Canadian literary magazines, on cbc Radio, and in *Rolling Stone*. He has one collection of poetry, *This Cabin As The SS Titanic,* and several chapbooks. Timothy Shay hosts two events for writers in Vancouver: Hogan's Alley Open Poetry Readings, which are held once a month at Hogan's Alley Cafe, and the Twisted Poets Literary Salon, a Pandora's Collective event held at the Prophouse Cafe twice each month.

Poet, critic and literary journalist **Trevor Carolan** has travelled internationally for more than thirty years, writing on art, literature, music, politics, and Asian cultures. His publications include many books and his work has appeared in five languages. He teaches English and Creative Writing at University of the Fraser Valley, British Columbia.

All poems are published with permission of the poet, in addition to the permission of any previous publisher, as cited below.

VANCOUVER

"After the Tsunami," Robin Susanto. Reprinted with permission from *Quills Canadian Poetry*

"a lightness dances," Diane Tucker. Reprinted with permission from *Bright Scarves of Hours*. Kingsville, ON: Palimpsest Press, 1997.

"Appleton," Heather Haley. Reprinted with permission from *Three Blocks West of Wonderland*. Victoria, BC: Ekstasis Editions, 2009.

"Attempts to Know the Past," Aislinn Hunter. Reprinted with permission from *The Possible Past*. Richmond, BC: Raincoast Books, 2005.

"Beer, Blood, & Bukowski," Shannon Rayne. Reprinted from *Poetry is Dead, Issue 3*. poetryisdead.ca

"Border Boogie (1969)," Susan McCaslin. Reprinted with permission from Allan Briesmaster, ed., *Crossing Lines: Poets who Came to Canada in the Vietnam Era*, Toronto: Seraphim Editions, 2008, and *Demeter Goes Skydiving*, Edmonton, AB: University of Alberta Press, 2011.

"Cabin Fever," Anna Swanson. Reprinted with permisson from *the Night's Also*. Toronto: Tightrope Books, 2010.

"Cell Phone," Christopher Levenson. Reprinted with permission from *Local Time*. Ottawa, ON: Stone Flower Press, 2006.

"Crows," Sandy Shreve. Reprinted with permission from *Suddenly So Much*. Holstein, ON: Exile Editions, 2005.

"Desdamona (Durga)," Joanne Arnott. First appeared in *The New Chief Tongue*, chieftongue.blogspot.com/

"Everyday things," Lilija Valis. Reprinted with permission from *Freedom on the Fault Line*. Parker, CO: Outskirts Press, 2012.

"The Goodnight Skirt," Raoul Fernandes. Originally published as "In the Treehouse." Reprinted from *Emerge 2009*.

"Hollow," David Zieroth. Reprinted with permission from *The Fly in Autumn*, Harbour Publishing, 2009, www.harbourpublishing.com.

"Manning Park in the Dark," Evelyn Lau. Reprinted with permission from *Living Under Plastic*. Fernie, BC: Oolichan, 2010.

"mount pleasant," Nikki Reimer. Reprinted with permission from *[sic]*. Calgary, AB: Frontenac House, 2010.

"Nadine," Russell Thornton. Reprinted with permission from *The Human Shore*, Harbour Publishing, 2006, www.harbourpublishing.com.

"the next growing season: a glossary," Renée Sarojini Saklikar. Reprinted with permission from *thecanadaproject.com*.

"Offering," Rita Wong, *forage*, Nightwood Editions, 2007, www.nightwoodeditions.com

"Our Salt Spring Island Dinner," Chris Gilpin. Originally printed in *Contemporary Verse 2*, www.contemporaryverse2.ca/

"Rushing Undergrowth," Kate Braid. Reprinted with permission from *To This Cedar Fountain*. Halfmoon Bay, BC: Caitlin Press, 2012.

"Stealing Anatomies," Kraljii Elee Gardiner. Reprinted with permission from *The Writers Caravan Anthology* Vancouver, BC: Otter Press, 2011.

"The Stone," Ibrahim Honjo. Reprinted with permission from *Roots in the Stone*. Markham, ON: Books, Inc., 1990.

"Tongue," Susan Cormier. Reprinted with permission from *All Wound Up*. Vancouver, BC: Ripple Effect Press, 2002.

"The Wailing Machine," Rob Taylor. Reprinted with permission from *The Other Side of Ourselves*. Markham, ON: Cormorant Books, 2011.

"The Weight of Dew," Daniela Elza. Reprinted with permission from *The Weight of Dew*. Salt Spring Island, BC: Mother Tongue Publishing, 2012.

"What we heard about the Canadians," Rachel Rose. Originally appeared in *Rattle*, #35, Summer 2011, www.rattle.com/poetry/print/30s/i35/

ACKNOWLEDGEMENTS

Ooligan Press takes its name from a Native American word for the OOLIGAN PRESS common smelt or candlefish. Ooligan is a general trade press rooted in the rich literary life of Portland and the Department of English at Portland State University. Ooligan is staffed by students pursuing master's degrees in an apprenticeship program under the guidance of a core faculty of publishing professionals.

Acquisitions
Tony Anderson
J. Adam Collins
John Sibley Williams

Permissions
Katie Allen
Heather Frazier
Tara Lehmann
Jonathan Stark
Kristen Svenson

Editors
Katie Allen
Kylie Byrd
Gino Cerruti
Heather Frazier
Rachel Hanson
Rebekah Hunt
Tiah Lindner
Amber May
Isaac Mayo
Anne Paulsen
Ashley Rogers
Jonathan Stark
Kristen Svenson
Jennifer Tibbett
Amreen Ukani
Amanda Winterroth

Cover Design
J. Adam Collins

Interior Design
Poppy Milliken
Lorna Nakell

Miscellaneous Design
Brandon Freels
Mandi Russell
Kelsey Yocum

Online materials
Kate Burkett

E-book Design
Kai Belladone
Anna Smith

Logo Design
Tristen Jackman
Lisa Shaffer

Marketing & Sales
Emily Gravlin
Kristin Howe
Kathryn Ostendorff

Project Management
J. Adam Collins
Joel Eisenhower
Amber May
Tina Morgan
Kathryn Ostendorff
Rachel Pass
Jessica Snavlin
Jonathan Stark
John Sibley Williams

OOLIGAN
P R E S S

369 Neuberger Hall
724 SW Harrison Street
Portland, Oregon 97201
Phone: 503.725.9748 | Fax: 503.725.3561
ooligan@ooliganpress.pdx.edu | ooligan.pdx.edu

Ooligan Press is a general trade publisher rooted in the rich literary tradition of the Pacific Northwest. A region widely recognized for its unique and innovative sensibilities, this small corner of America is one of the most diverse in the United States, comprising urban centers, small towns, and wilderness areas. Its residents range from ranchers, loggers, and small business owners to scientists, inventors, and corporate executives. From this wealth of culture, Ooligan Press aspires to discover works that reflect the values and attitudes that inspire so many to call the Northwest their home.

Founded in 2001, Ooligan is a teaching press dedicated to the art and craft of publishing. Affiliated with Portland State University, the press is staffed by students pursuing master's degrees in an apprenticeship program under the guidance of a core faculty of publishing professionals.

Ordering information:

Individual Sales: All Ooligan Press titles are available through your local bookstore, and we encourage supporting independent booksellers. Please contact your local bookstore, or purchase online through Powell's, Indiebound, or Amazon.

Retail Sales: Ooligan books are distributed to the trade through Ingram Publisher Services. Booksellers and businesses that wish to stock Ooligan titles may order directly from IPS at (866) 400-5351 or customerservice@ingrampublisherservices.com.

Educational and Library Sales: We sell directly to educators and libraries that do not have an established relationship with IPS. For pricing, or to place an order, please contact us at operations@ooliganpress.pdx.edu.

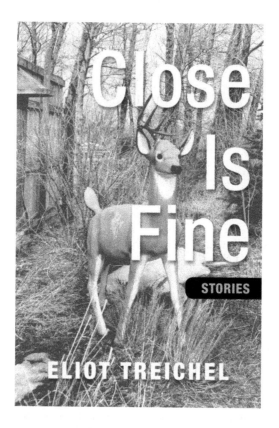

Close Is Fine

a short story collection
by Eliot Treichel

fiction | 168 pages | $14.95
5½" × 8½" | softcover | ISBN: 978-1-932010-45-9

OOLIGAN
P R E S S

Like a Polaroid snapshot, this finely wrought collection of short stories gives us a brief glimpse into the quirky and complex lives of rural town inhabitants. As the characters struggle to define their individuality and reconcile their ideals with ordinary life, we are witness to their unique self-discoveries. At times mournful and haunting, this story collection celebrates the nobility of simple life, of striving and failing without ever losing hope.

Ooligan Press • Portland, Oregon • ooligan.pdx.edu

Available May 2013 from Ooligan Press

Up Nights

a novel
by Daniel Kine

fiction | $13.95 | 200 pages
5" × 8" | softcover | ISBN: 978-1-932010-63-3

OOLIGAN
PRESS

Up Nights Daniel Kine's second book, is a classic road novel for a new generation. In raw, unrelenting prose, Kine tells the story of the complexities of human relationships when four friends embark on an existential journey through the underbelly of society. As they drift from city to city, they each struggle to connect with the disenchanted people they encounter along the way. *Up Nights* speaks to the reality of the human condition: the unequivocal impermanence of life.

Ooligan Press • Portland, Oregon • ooligan.pdx.edu

American Scream: Palindrome Apocalypse

by Dubravka Oraić Tolić

poetry | $14.95
240 pages | 6" × 9" | softcover
ISBN: 978-1-93-2010-10-7

Utopia—we all want our own, but who pays for it
and at what price? Croatian poet Dubravka Oraić
Tolić delivers a masterful, thought-provoking answer
with exquisite language and imagery in the epic poem *American Scream*.
Complementing *American Scream* is *Palindrome Apocalypse*—a palindrome
that is artful in both technique and story—presented side-by-side with the
Croatian original to preserve its visual effect. Together, Oraić Tolić's poems
explore dark themes of social and individual selfishness in pursuit of dreams and
the unintended consequences of those efforts; examine the tension between
a nation's dream of freedom and the outworking of that dream; capture the
heart of pre- and post-war Croatia, yet speak universally of the pain of bring-
ing one's visions to life.

Dot-to-Dot, Oregon

by Sid Miller

poetry | $13.95
88 pages | 6" × 9" | softcover
ISBN: 978-1-93-2010-29-9

Sid Miller explores seven routes from the coast
to the mountains, from inner-city Portland to the
Idaho border. *Dot-to-Dot, Oregon*, a collection of
fifty poems, travels through the cities, towns, and
monuments of Oregon. Using these locales as a background, three voices nar-
rate the author's loving but critical relationship with the state he calls home.

"Connect the dots? If you do you'll discover some strange and wonderful constella-
tions superimposed over familiar topography... *Dot-to-Dot* is a lyrical and, at times,
a dark and hilarious guide to the blue lines (secondary roads) of the Beaver State.
So before you head out to Shoetree (Don't look for it on a highway map.), Nyssa (a
damsel in metaphysical distress?), or some other exotic location in the Beaver State,
take a look at Sid Miller's new book or, better yet, take it with you on your rambles."

— Carlos Reyes

Ooligan Press • Portland, Oregon • ooligan.pdx.edu

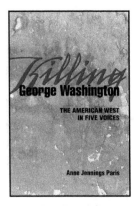

Killing George Washington:
The American West in Five Voices
by Anne Jennings Paris

poetry | $13.95
120 pages | 6" × 9" | softcover
ISBN: 978-1-93-2010-30-5

Killing George Washington tells the story of the American frontier as it moves west. Anne Jennings Paris, in a collection of narrative poems, imagines the voices of the forgotten historical figures of Lewis Wetzel, a notorious Indian killer; York, the slave who accompanied Lewis and Clark; Charity Lamb, Oregon's first convicted murderess; Ing Hay, a Chinese immigrant who made a name for himself as a doctor; and Mary Colter, an architect who helped shaped the western landscape. Exploring the American consciousness, these poems question our shared heritage through the personal stories of legends.

Oregon Stories
Edited by Ooligan Press

poetry | $16.95
272 pages | 6" × 9" | softcover
ISBN: 978-1-932010-33-6

This collection of 150 personal narratives from everyday Oregonians explores the thoughts, feelings, and experiences of the people who live in this unique state. *Oregon Stories* shows why people cherish this state and why Oregonians strive to keep Oregon unique and beautiful while celebrating its rich history and diverse opportunities. Drawn from the Oregon 150 Commission's Oregon Stories website project—in which a variety of citizens submitted personal stories that will resonate with any Oregon resident—this book collects the stories and histories of the people that make this place home. The subject of these stories varies widely—some authors tell detailed family histories, while others describe exciting travels throughout Oregon's beautiful landscape. This book features local contributors who reside in different communities all over the state, resulting in a publication truly representative of Oregonians as a whole. Read much more about the Oregon Stories project as part of the Oregon 150 Official Sesquicentennial Commemoration on the main website.

Ooligan Press • Portland, Oregon • ooligan.pdx.edu

You Have Time for This:

Contemporary American Short-Short Stories

Edited by Mark Budman & Tom Hazuka

fiction | $11.95
135 pages | 5" × 7½" | softcover
ISBN: 978-1932010-17-6

Love, death, fantasy, and foreign lands, told with brevity and style by the best writers in the short-short fiction genre. *You Have Time for This* satiates your craving for fine literature without making a dent in your schedule. This collection takes the modern reader on fifty-three literary rides, each one only five hundred words or less. Mark Budman and Tom Hazuka, two of the top names in the genre, have compiled an anthology of mini-worlds are as diverse as the authors who created them. Contributing writers include Steve Almond, author of *My Life in Heavy Metal* and *Candyfreak*; Aimee Bender, author of *The Girl in the Flammable Skirt*; Robert Boswell, author of five novels, including *Century's Son*; Alex Irvine, author of *A Scattering of Jades*; L. E. Leone, who writes a weekly humorous column about food and life for the *San Francisco Bay Guardian*; Justine Musk, author of dark-fantasy novels, including *Blood Angel*; Susan O'Neill, writer of nonfiction and fiction with a book of short stories called *Don't Mean Nothing*; *Short Stories of Vietnam*; and Katharine Weber, author of several novels, including *Triangle*. From Buddha to beer, sex to headless angels, there's a story here for everyone. In *You Have Time for This* you will find: flash fiction from forty-four authors, works from across the globe, highly regarded authors from all types of genres, fresh work from emerging writers, and fifty-three stand alone pieces that tie the world together.

Enjoy. You have time for this.

"A really good flash fiction is like a story overheard at a bar—personal, funny, dangerous, and sometimes hard to believe. *You Have Time for This* distills those qualities and many others into quick tall tales by writers who are as talented as they are magical."

—Kevin Sampsell, author of *Beautiful Blemish* and publisher of Future Tense Publishing

Ooligan Press • Portland, Oregon • ooligan.pdx.edu

Write to Publish

annual publishing conference hosted by

OOLIGAN
P R E S S

http://ooligan.pdx.edu/w2p/

Write to Publish is unlike any writing conference you've previously attended. Instead of focusing on the craft of writing, we explore the process of getting published.

The panels will host a variety of authors who will speak about their own experiences in publishing. These topic-led discussions are intended as an "industry mingle" with a Q & A. The authors will focus on the ups and downs, challenges, and triumphs they experienced in their careers. Local vendors from the publishing industry will also be present, sharing their knowledge and services with conference-goers.

Write to Publish is about empowering you as a writer so that you are one step closer to getting published. Get ready to spend a day having your questions answered and seeing how you, too, can become a published author.

Ooligan Press • Portland, Oregon • ooligan.pdx.edu

Printed in the USA
CPSIA information can be obtained
at www.ICGtesting.com
JSHW012055140824
68134JS00035B/3463

9 781932 010534